Reasons to Be Pretty

Neil LaBute received his Master of Fine Arts degree in dramatic writing from New York University and was the recipient of a literary fellowship to study at the Royal Court Theatre, London. He also attended the Sundance Institute's Playwrights Lab and is the Playwright-in-Residence with MCC Theatre in New York City.

LaBute's plays include: *bash: latter-day plays*, *The Shape of Things*, *The Mercy Seat*, *The Distance From Here*, *Autobahn*, *Fat Pig* (Olivier Award nominated for Best Comedy), *Some Girl(s)*, *This Is How It Goes*, *Wrecks*, *Filthy Talk for Troubled Times*, *In a Dark Dark House*, *Reasons to Be Pretty* (Tony Award nominated for Best Play) and *The Break of Noon*. In the spring of 2011 his play *In a Forest, Dark and Deep* premiered in London's West End. LaBute is also the author of *Seconds of Pleasure*, a collection of short fiction which was published by Grove Atlantic.

His films include *In the Company of Men* (New York Critics' Circle Award for Best First Feature and the Filmmaker Trophy at the Sundance Film Festival), *Your Friends and Neighbors*, *Nurse Betty*, *Possession*, *The Shape of Things*, a film adaptation of his play of the same title, *The Wicker Man*, *Lakeview Terrace* and *Death at a Funeral*.

NEIL LABUTE

Reasons to Be Pretty

faber and faber

This edition first published in 2011
by Faber and Faber Limited
74–77 Great Russell Street
London WC1B 3DA

Originally published in the USA by Faber and Faber Inc in 2008

Typeset by Country Setting, Kingsdown, Kent CT14 8ES
Printed and bound by CPI Group (UK) Ltd, Croydon, CR0 4YY

A CIP record for this book
is available from the British Library

978-0-571-28069-8

8 10 9

Introduction

Name the asshole who first invented mirrors.

I'm not actually posing that question, as I could quickly find out on my own by using my handy Google button or whipping over to Wikipedia, but I haven't bottomed out that far as a writer (or a human being) quite yet. I still like to look things up for myself occasionally, even cracking open an old leather-bound edition of encyclopedias from time to time to get a piece of information. I know some-body invented mirrors – they exist, after all; no doubt someone's ancestors are taking credit for the discovery – but I'm asking in a more general way, a sort of 'Why did they bother?' Do we really need to see ourselves that clearly? Or at all? We see others for who they are – physically, at least – and yet we never actually see ourselves outright, always catching a glance in a window's reflection or in the glimmer off a lake's placid surface. But we want more. We want to know what we really look like, what people really think of us; if we're pretty enough, good enough, the best. We are creatures of desire – we want all the time. It's end-less, how much we crave things – compliments and cars and lotto tickets (because if we win we'll have a lot of money, and then we can get more stuff) – and so we work and spend time away from our loved ones, always telling our-selves that this is the way of the world and everybody does it and my kids want it, and so life slips away. You attend your school of choice (if you're lucky), and you get your job of choice (if you're lucky), and you slave away at it until it's time to retire and somebody else takes your desk two days after you leave, and you go to Florida a few times, and then you're done. Gone. What will you leave behind, dear reader? Something, I hope.

Every so often I think that all that'll remain when I've left this place is two great kids and six inches of library space taken up by my published works. There is a lovely line in A. S. Byatt's novel *Possession* that sums it up very well: 'To a dusty shelf we aspire.' We writers stare into a variety of mirrors, studying the faces of people we don't yet know as we make them up, working to create a series of believable psychological profiles for a bunch of folks who don't really exist. I prefer it to life most of the time, as it's much safer and a whole lot easier. These 'people' all seem to be the same as us, unfortunately – my flaws become theirs and their wants and loves grow out of my own, and suddenly I'm surrounded by the same miserable, lovely, lonely, sad, terrific people that I was escaping from in the first place. And all these characters stare in their own mirrors and wonder if they too are good and pretty and smart and liked. Or at least good and pretty and smart and liked enough. Am I just pretty enough? Enough to get by and not be laughed at, and to meet someone and be happy? All because we can't be sure, having never really seen ourselves. Those damn mirrors are of absolutely no use to us, in the end. They tell us exactly what we wish to hear – everything, in fact, but the truth. What is it to be 'pretty'? It's not beautiful, and it's certainly not ugly. Why do we care about it so much? Why do we get so caught up in what other people think? Probably for the same reasons we use Google and laugh along when somebody tells a joke that we don't get and continue to go into debt but keep these stupid smiles plastered on our faces. Because we're deathly afraid of being singled out for being anything but normal. We go to high school for three or four years, but it colours our entire lives – we continue to live some version of its schedules and cliques for the rest of our natural days. In school we were all desperate to fit in and yet desperate to stand out; the rest of life is merely a variation of all that. It's a deadly game of push-pull.

If I could be anything but a writer – and I can't, I've tried – I would be a braver person. One who just doesn't give two shits about what other people say or think or feel; I don't think that would make me callous or uncaring or stuck-up (to utilise a wonderfully high-schoolish word). I think it would simply make me hold my head up a little higher, look people in the eye for a bit longer, make my smile a little broader (and any picture of me will attest that smiling is not my strong suit). I hope this play makes a case for being yourself and standing up for what you believe in. For being brave. For making choices that are hard and adult and not easy. For going out and being a part of the world instead of a mere observer. I've written about a lot of men who are really little boys at heart, but Greg, the protagonist in this play, just might be one of the few adults I've ever tackled. The play talks a bit about our country's (and, by extension, the world's) obsession with physical beauty, but it's really the first coming-of-age story I've written. A boy grows up and becomes a man. I suppose every writer has one of those stories to tell, and this one is mine. It also concerns a very blue-collar side of the work population, like the friends and family I grew up with. I know what a dead-end job is like. I know exactly what it's like to be eating your lunch at 3:00 a.m. and feeling like life as you know it is now officially over. I have a profound respect for work and workers and communities who live from pay cheque to pay cheque. The worst day I've had writing is better than the best day I ever had working in a factory, and the people who do it, year after year, because that's life, and food and rent and child support must be paid, have all my respect. Writing is easy. Life is hard. It's more than hard – it's a bitch (as many bumper stickers are happy to point out for us). I suppose that's why I like the person who spends more time working than on Facebook, the person who gets out there and lives his life rather than blogging about it or staring in the mirror wondering about anything so damn inconsequential as looks or hair or yesterday. The future is now. It's time to grow up and be strong. Tomorrow may well be too late.

Neil LaBute, 2008

Looking Forward to the Past

Even as you read this life has moved on. And again. And yet again.

We're so busy living for the future that we rarely appreciate today until it becomes the past. Not exactly groundbreaking philosophy, I know, but at least it's kind of true. So many things in my life have happened without me fully appreciating them (or worse, letting others know I've appreciated them) and then, to add insult to injury, the moment is gone. In the past. Vanished.

It's the same with my work. I often find myself looking forward to that next film or theatrical production even while something else is up and playing to audiences – it's such a human thing (or at least an American thing) always to be reaching for what's next, what's new, what's ahead. If you're not careful, it's very easy to get caught up in that movement and to undervalue all that you've already been given or done or had.

A moment like this one – a play getting another production at a wonderful venue – is a pretty good reason to stop and smell the proverbial roses. I've had this chance before and with the same director, Michael Attenborough, to rethink a play of mine and to polish all the bits that needed attending to. I was very happy with *Reasons to Be Pretty* when it arrived off-Broadway and even in its Broadway incarnation (although I'm excited to be restoring the original 'A moment with . . .' monologues to the play, as I feel that they contribute to the thematic debate if not the plot itself). We have also cut and pasted and even added a few new things, including allowing Carly to be pregnant throughout the play rather than us finding out this news deep in the second act.

Mike has given me lots of food for thought as did my original director, Terry Kinney, before him and it's made me a better writer. I don't like getting pushed around and bullied – that happened enough to me when I was a kid – but sometimes it helps an artist to hear 'no' and 'not good enough' a few times. It wakes you up and makes you dig in a bit, or at least it does me. The quartet of great actors at the Almeida asked hard questions just like their American counterparts did and the play is that much better now as a result – I love how theatre, while ephemeral, is a living thing and a play can continue to grow through each incarnation. I'm not doing this to create a bunch of museum exhibits – if I'm successful at all it's because I keep trying to grab the audience by their collective lapels (it's much harder if they are wearing T-shirts) and give them fresh new voices and characters and situations to deal with.

While the play itself is deeply American in its lingo and people, I hope that there is a universal message buried in the laughs and anger and heartbreak. I always seem to be able to count on English audiences to tell me when I hit on the truth or if I'm just scribbling down a bunch of bullshit. The English are great at spotting bullshit (well, with the possible exception of Neville Chamberlain).

And if I do end up just writing bullshit, then I'm going to make sure that it's the most progressive, provocative bullshit it can be.

And that's a promise, my friends.

Neil LaBute, 2011

Reasons to Be Pretty was first performed at the Lucille Lortel Theatre, New York City, on 2 June 2008, in a production by the Manhattan Class Company (MCC). The cast was as follows:

Greg Thomas Sadoski
Steph Alison Pill
Kent Pablo Schreiber
Carly Piper Perabo

Director Terry Kinney
Scenic Designer David Gallo
Lighting David Weiner
Sound Designers Robert Milburn and Michael Bodeen
Costume Designer Sarah J. Holden

Reasons to Be Pretty was first performed in London at the Almeida Theatre on 10 November 2011. The cast was as follows:

Greg Tom Burke
Steph Siân Brooke
Kent Kieran Bew
Carly Billie Piper

Director Michael Attenborough
Design Soutra Gilmour
Lighting Mark Henderson
Sound Fergus O'Hare
Dialect Penny Dyer
Fight Director Terry King

Characters

Greg

Steph

Kent

Carly

*A slash (/) indicates the point of overlap
in interrupted dialogue*

REASONS TO BE PRETTY

Act One

Lights burst on.
  At home. Two people in their bedroom, already deep in the middle of it. A nice little fight. Wham!

Greg . . . No, no, no, no, no, uh-uh, no!

Steph Yes!

Greg No, that's not it! / I didn't say that!

Steph Don't lie, you fucker! / Yes, you did!

Greg Steph . . .

Steph No, don't, do not 'Steph' me right now!

Greg . . . Come on, Stephanie . . .

Steph Don't do *that*, you prick! Don't play the 'Stephanie' game, do not do it!!

Greg But I didn't say anything, I'm telling you the truth here! And I *definitely* didn't use that word, so . . . that's . . .

Steph Bullshit!

Greg I didn't! I would never say that about you, *ever*, and I'm not gonna be . . .

Steph Bullshit!! / BULLSHIT! Fucker . . .

Greg I did not, I don't care what she said to you . . . / I didn't say 'ugly'! No. I'm . . .

Steph She was in the other room, you bastard! In the *next* room, OK, so don't try and Lance Armstrong your way outta this one!

3

Greg I'm not! / I barely mentioned you, that's all. In a *nice* way. It wasn't, like, some big . . .

Steph Back-pedalling like some . . . / Fuck you.

Greg Look, God, I just wanna go to . . . bed . . .

Steph . . . I don't care what you wanna do. Dick.

Greg OK, would you stop, please? / Steph . . .

Steph I'm not gonna stop, no, for what? Huh?! What for? / For *you*? Fuck that.

Greg No, because I'm, so I can explain the . . .

Steph You don't need to, I've already heard all the explanations I wanna hear and I don't believe you. You get that? / I-do-not-ever-believe-the-shit-that-comes-out-of-your-mouth. *Ever*.

Greg Yes. / Yeah, well, that's fucked. OK?

Steph No, you're fucked, that's what's fucked here, mister, you are . . . you are fucked. Big time.

Greg This is just stupid, so I'm not gonna . . .

Steph Don't do it! Do not walk out of here when we're fighting or I swear to God I'll . . . I will murder your fish when you're gone. I'll flush them or I'll, I'll do whatever it takes but I will *hurt* you and you will not like it! That's what I'll do so you'd better just stay right there – no, I don't want you to come over and hold me, God no – but you better stay around and argue this shit out or I'm gonna . . . wreck your life a little bit. Swear I fucking will – I don't care if I'm late going in or not. So.

> *They both stop for a moment, letting this sink in. Steph angrily piles her hair into a makeshift bun-type thing.*

Greg Man, this is . . . You're talking nuts now. / Seriously.

Steph Don't say that, either. / I mean, boy, if you're looking for things to get shitty, then OK, but otherwise I wouldn't say a thing like that, not anything about being psycho or that sorta junk. / Uh-uh. No.

Greg Stephanie, listen . . . / *Please* . . .

Steph Fuck 'please'. Please is shit. Please is like something you crap out in your pants and are too embarrassed to clean up . . . I'm not gonna even listen to 'please'. No.

Greg OK, then, I don't know what to say to you about this . . . because . . .

Steph The truth. I might be willing to overlook your general fuckheadedness if I felt as if the truth might be on its way at some point here . . .

Greg I'm telling you the . . . whole . . .

Steph Don't say it if it's not because I will know and you know that I'll know. You'll know it and I will pounce on you like I was death itself if you're lying to me . . . Seriously. Like fucking death.

Greg Ya know, you swear a lot when you're mad.

Steph Fuck. You. / Cocksucker.

Greg See? / I'm just saying . . .

Steph And I'm saying 'fuck you'. If that's all you can do right now, try and dilute the issue at hand by sidetracking us . . . / Or getting us all turned around by . . .

Greg . . . I'm just pointing it out . . . / I'm not, I *swear* I'm not, but you're being all . . .

Steph . . . Or, or trying to make me smile or any of that shit that you usually do, then 'fuck you' is what I have to say! To you.

Greg . . . Fine then.

Steph Yeah, fine.

Greg OK.

Steph O-kay. Don't you fucking laugh at me. (*Beat.*) So?

Greg *What?* And don't you have to be at work?

Steph Don't deflect me, asshole . . .

Greg I'm *not*! I'm just trying to be . . .

Steph What did you say that she heard and then called me about? / Hmm? What?

Greg I didn't . . . / God . . .

Steph I'm telling you the truth about what I'll do to you. I am.

Greg Steph . . .

Steph *Greg* . . .

Greg I really didn't say anything! (*Beat.*) It's not, I mean, did she say that I . . . ? What?

Steph You don't remember? Hmm?

Greg No. I mean, I was talking to Kent and we were laughing about stuff, about, like, I dunno – work and how this new guy who's a real goof has been begging us to join our baseball team so we're joking about whatever and . . . that's all. / Come *on*, Steph, you know how we are when we get . . .

Steph Yeah? / What?

Greg Just *talking*!! Jesus. Going on about our lives and situations and . . . / Nothing! It's no big deal, anything we said, and if she is gonna call you every time I open up my mouth over at their place, then I'm never gonna go there again! Alright? I'm not . . .

Steph *And?* / Wow, bet she'll be crushed.

Greg I'm just saying . . . I'm sick of her acting like a cop even when she's off duty. She isn't one, OK, she's *not*. / She's a – it's basically like being a hall monitor.

Steph Fine then. / And so you're *talking* . . .

Greg Honey, come on . . . don't be all . . .

Steph No, tell me. Tell me what you said.

Greg I didn't say any—

Steph About me. You said it loud enough for her to hear it, for her to repeat it to me in complete detail – *verbatim*, as you like to call it – so you can say it to my face . . .

Greg Oh . . . fuck . . .

Steph Nope, that wasn't it. (*Beat.*) Go on.

Greg Stephanie, stop it . . .

Steph You want me to say it? How 'bout if we do it that way – I say it to you and you tell me if it's true or not?

Greg I'm not, no . . . that's stupid, so no.

Steph You sure? Maybe it's easier that way – treat you like a *pre*-schooler.

Greg I don't need anything to be *easier*, OK, I don't . . . Look, I'm not scared of you or about anything I said because it wasn't a big deal; we'd had a few beers and maybe we're a bit loud out in the garage where we were talking, but I didn't say . . . shit.

Steph She was in the kitchen, Greg. Door to the kitchen was open. Voices travel. They're made up of *sound*, case you didn't know . . .

Greg Yeah, I'm down with the basic scientific principles, Steph, thanks very much.

Steph And so she's cooking up some ground beef for tacos on the stove and she hears you, plain as day, going on about me and there is no doubt in her mind – that's *none*, no doubt of any kind – that you said exactly what she repeated to me . . .

Greg I see. (*Beat.*) Over the sound of *hot* meat she can hear me talking?

Steph . . . Awwwww, you're so . . . / You asshole . . .

Greg I'm just asking! / Don't I get to ask any shit here or is it just a one-sided deal we got going now?

Steph Don't be a complete dick, alright? *Don't.* I know that's your soup of the *jour* but, please, just give me a little . . .

Greg Fine! So she can hear me talking – she's suddenly like Wonder Woman or something and from an entire room away she hears me and what I'm saying to Kent as we're out there banging away on his Chevelle. Is that it?

Steph You mean the Bionic Woman, not Wonder Woman – who had various powers but hearing wasn't one of 'em – I mean, of course she could hear, she wasn't deaf, but not in any special way. The *Bionic* Woman had the super hearing . . . smart guy . . .

Greg Whatever! You know what I mean . . .

Steph I do, yeah, that's why I just corrected you on it. / *Bionic* Woman. Lindsay Wagner.

Greg Great. / Thanks.

Steph Doesn't matter, you're just deflecting it again . . . *Yes*, she heard you guys, clear as day. / Or a bell, or whatever . . .

Greg Fine. / OK, and? *And?*

Steph What?

Greg What'd she say? I mean, that I said?

Steph Oh, so *now* you want me to say it . . .

Greg If you need to so bad . . .

Steph I thought you didn't want me to, thought you said it was stupid.

Greg That was before . . .

Steph 'Before'?

Greg Yeah, before.

Steph 'Before' what?

Greg *Before* . . . you pissed me off.

Steph Oh. Oh, I see . . . (*Beat.*) Before I pissed you off? *You're* pissed off now?! Fucker! / God, you are such a prick, Greg . . .

Greg And again with the mouth. / Stop!! My God, you're like an *Eddie Murphy* concert or something . . . with all the . . .

Steph Fuck you, asswipe! AHHHH!!

Greg Can we not make the *entire* building aware of your psychotic break with reality?

Steph Fuck you, fuck you, FUCK YOU! FUCK *YOU*!!

Greg OK, you know what, I don't need to stand here and take this . . . I don't. Throw the fish in the toilet again, it's not like I'm gonna be surprised – I'm not about to hang out here and get abused like this. / I'm not. (*Beat.*) You've got a real issue with your temper there, Steph . . .

Steph No, don't you . . . / Don't you *even* . . .

Greg I'm sorry but it's true – you're acting crazy now! Like a fucking nutcase!

Steph Shut up, fuckhead. / You fucker . . .

Greg I mean it. / You're crazy – a goddamn loon!

Steph Tell me what you said. / TELL ME, I just want you to say it and then I'll stop!

Greg No . . . / No, you're . . . *What* is up with you?!

Steph Say it! / SAY IT!!

Greg It's not . . . / I didn't say . . . How did this happen, why are you such a freak? I mean, this is like a *serious* personality glitch you've got there . . .

Steph SAY IT TO ME, SAY IT! / SAY IT NOW!!

Greg Stephanie, stop it or I'll call the cops myself, I will. / STOP! (*Beat.*) It'll be me this time, OK, not the neighbours! I'm not kidding around here!! Seriously . . .

Steph THEN SAY IT! SAY IT. (*Dead calm.*) Just do it and I will quit.

   Greg waits for a moment, gathers himself. Steph watching his every move. Coiled.

Greg Fine. / (*Checks watch.*) It's quarter of . . .

Steph Fine. / Prick . . . do it. GO!

Greg I will. / I'm going to . . . Jesus . . .

Steph Then-do-it. / Then . . .

Greg . . . Stop. OK? Just stop. (*Beat.*) Kent said something about a new girl at work, some younger gal who just got hired – she's not in our division but over in the shipping office, works swing shift – and he thought she was *hot*. Said she was pretty and I agreed and that was all. Really. / Yeah.

Steph That's it? / Huh.

Greg No big deal. I mean, look . . . he's always had an eye for, you know . . . BUT I WAS just going along WITH IT . . . (*Beat.*) And I don't know why she's gotta be saying something about *me*, stirring up trouble . . . I mean, fuck, I wasn't the guy talking shit about some other – you know. I mean, think about that. OK? Just . . . ask yourself *that* question. (*Beat.*) Now maybe she just doesn't wanna face it – 'reality', I'm saying – because she's carrying his kid or whatever, but hey, that's not *my* problem. Right?

Steph I see. (*Beat.*) And nothing about me?

Greg I'm . . . / I don't think I said any—

Steph You didn't say anything about me compared to her? Nothing? / No?

Greg . . . No. No, not in *comparison* or . . . / Nope.

Steph Or anything like that? At all? / You got this far, don't fuck it up now . . .

Greg I said . . . no, what I said was, I know what I said now . . . This is it. I said this. It was, like, umm, 'Yeah, well, maybe Steph hasn't got a face like that girl's – maybe her face is just *regular* – but I wouldn't trade her for a million bucks.' Something like that. / You know . . . / I was just . . .

Steph Oh. / Ahhhh. / 'Regular.'

Greg Yeah. That was all . . . I'm . . . yes. *Regular.*

Steph OK.

Greg See? I never said 'ugly'. / I just . . .

Steph Uh-huh. / Yep. That's what Carly said to me you said. Those *exact* words.

Greg Alright then. Which was not meant as any sort of comparison. / It wasn't.

Steph No? / Really?

Greg At all! It was more of, like, a point of contrast – with *you* as the good thing.

Steph Huh. (*Beat.*) Even though *she*'s beautiful?

Greg 'Pretty.' Yeah. Steph, it was meant as a *compliment*. It was. / Honestly.

Steph I see . . . / A 'compliment'. Well, guess what?

> *Steph gathers herself and heads to the door. Picks up an ashtray and fires it across the room at Greg. Just misses him and smashes against the wall.*

It's fucking not!

> *Steph storms out, leaving Greg alone in the room. He sits down on an ottoman and runs his hands through his hair. A slow shake of his head.*

Greg . . . Oh, boy.

SCENE TWO

At work.
> *Greg and Kent sitting around the break room of their workplace. In jumpsuits. Just finishing up their lunch – it's after midnight and they're both tired. Third-shifters.*

Kent . . . And then what?

Greg She left. Drove off. / Took *my* car . . .

Kent Wow. / Bitch.

Greg Yeah. To her parents' house or some crap like that, you know?

Kent Right.

Greg Making a statement.

Kent Exactly.

Greg Threw a chair at me, actually, and one of those pots, you know, with the handle on it . . .

Kent No, what?

Greg You know, where you make, like, pancakes and shit . . . you *know* . . .

Kent That's a pan. Frying pan. / Or *skillet*, if you wanna get fancy.

Greg Oh. / Yeah, well, one of those . . .

Kent Whoa. (*Beat.*) I thought you said a 'pot'.

Greg Whatever. It went whizzing by my head – I didn't exactly take stock, I ducked. Stuck my head in the kitchen and bam!

Kent Fuck. (*Beat.*) Just so you know, though . . . it's a pan.

Greg Fine! God . . .

Kent Dude, I used to work over at Denny's, so . . . I should know. 'S a 'pan'.

Greg OK, well, that's what she threw . . .

Kent And?

Greg And nothing. Haven't heard a word since. *Two* days.

Kent No?

Greg No call, a text, nothing. I rang up their place but I'm only getting the answering machine. (*Beat.*) Her mom's eating this up, I'm sure. She hates me . . .

Kent Figures.

13

Greg Yeah. Left a message, anyway. (*Beat.*) I'm just, like, totally *baffled* by this . . .

Kent nods and yawns – checks his watch. He slaps Greg on the back. Greg flinches as he opens up an energy snack.

Kent What's that?

Greg Power bar.

Kent Why're you having that?

Greg What d'you mean?

Kent You just had supper – now you're having one of those, too?

Greg Uh-huh. 'S the only way I'll make it to break—

Kent That doesn't make sense . . .

Greg They're good, though. Supposed to give y' a little jolt of energy.

Kent Yeah, but they're for, you know, like, as a supplement. If you don't have a meal or instead of – not after you already ate.

Greg Oh.

Kent They're not *dessert*. Even with all the chocolate on it . . .

Greg Huh. (*Beat.*) I think it's carob.

Kent Whatever! That's like having two meals.

Greg So? That's OK . . .

Kent I guess. If you wanna get fat it is . . .

Greg I'm not gonna get fat because I had one of these things – it's all natural stuff in it. Nuts and . . . I dunno. *Seeds.*

Kent You'd be surprised.

Greg Yeah, but . . . I mean, athletes eat 'em all the time. Olympians and whoever.

Kent Are you out running? Or swimming? Hmm? I don't see you doing cardio work or, like, lifting. Nothing. *Athletes* get away with that shit because they're always active, chipping away at their bodies. Not you. (*Beat.*) Shoving anything you find on the counter over there into your stomach . . .

Greg Kent, it's a fucking *snack*! Take it easy.

Kent Just pointing it out – got a group of guys counting on ya is all . . .

Greg Fine.

Kent And getting all chubby is not the way to win her back. / Or your face breaking out.

Greg Nice! / Thank you. (*Beat.*) *Shit* . . .

Kent Well . . . need you strong and fast for the team, man. Can't have any dead weight.

Greg That's really sensitive, thanks.

Kent Dude, it's for you – I'm throwing a little love your way, don't be a hater.

Greg Just shut up, OK? (*Beat.*) You got me out in *right* field. How good do I gotta be?

Kent Good enough to get us that motherfucking trophy! Huh? / (*Pumps his fist.*) Oh yeah!

Kent stands, points to a dusty shelf above the cabinets where several other trophies stand. Nothing very new.

Greg I guess . . . / Yep. (*Mock yell.*) Wooo–aa!

Kent Dude, come on! Be serious now . . . (*Beat.*) They haven't brought one a' those home since I started working here – last one was in, like, '86 or something. That's pathetic! (*He slaps the table and sits.*) *This* is the year! Without question.

> *Greg nods and pretends to cheer. He checks a wall clock against his watch.*

Greg (*yawns*) Third shift sucks.

Kent Yep. Pretty much. Even with the overtime . . .

Greg Agreed. (*Yawns.*) I'm *so* beat, man . . .

Kent 'Cept for that new girl. *Damn*, she's good looking! / *What*? / I'm just saying! She's a fox . . . *Love* to see if that carpet matches the curtains. (*Beat.*) I gotta take a dump.

Greg Ha! / You never change . . . / Go for it.

Kent Can't. I'm waiting for Carly – she's out on '*rounds*'. (*Grins.*) How gay is that?

Greg . . . Very. (*Beat.*) She pisses me off.

Kent Hey, man, don't blame her for this.

Greg I don't.

Kent Good, because you're the one who said it.

Greg I *know*. Shit! (*Beat.*) Course, she didn't need to jump on the phone and repeat it before I even got home, though, did she?

Kent Fuck, dude, she's a girl – they've got, like, *sonar*. It was a done deal, second it came outta your mouth.

Greg Yeah, well, she screwed me over but good. Steph is acting like . . . Crazy Horse . . .

Kent Exactly. Taking scalps . . .

Greg Yep.

Kent Noble savages my ass, right? (*Beat.*) They took people's *hair*! Fuckers . . .

Greg Uh-huh. (*Checks his watch.*) . . . Anyway, I'm just, you know, I'm saying that I'd never do something shitty like that to her. All *behind* her back and everything.

Kent Right. (*Beat.*) Fuck it, I'm gonna go.

Greg I'll wait for ya.

Kent Cool. (*Looks around.*) If she shows before I get back tell her I'm in the can . . .

Greg I'll probably flower it up a bit, but OK. Fine.

Kent nods and gathers up his trash, heading for the door. He dumps it – half goes on to the floor. He doesn't stop.
    Greg watches and shakes his head. Walks over with his own and tosses it; reaches down and collects the last of his buddy's mess, throws it out.
    Carly enters with her lunch but stops short when she sees Greg. She's wearing a full security uniform – the works. She is clearly pregnant.

Kent's using the restroom. I mean, in case you're wondering.

Carly Oh.

Greg He'll be back in a second. (*Beat.*) Tried to wait but, you know. Nature calls.

Carly 'Kay. Thanks.

She starts to leave again, then turns back. Sits down at a table and begins to nibble on a packaged item.
    Greg keeps his distance – circles around towards a window to have a look out. Reaches into his pocket for a book. Carly is watching him so Greg holds it up for her.

Greg It's Poe. / Oh. (*Nods.*) 'S pretty dark . . .

Carly I dunno who that is. / Yeah. Well, it's night out.

Greg Right. (*Smiles.*) No, I meant that my . . . what he writes about is . . .

Carly So it's gonna be . . . you know. Dark.

Greg . . . Yep. (*Decides to let it go.*) 'S true.

Carly That's why they call it that.

Greg What? Call what that?

Carly Night. / 'Cause it gets dark at night, so.

Greg Oh. / Is that why?

Carly I believe so . . .

Greg Huh. (*Beat.*) That doesn't really make any sense . . .

Carly No?

Greg I mean, not really . . . they could call it 'siesta' and it'd still be dark out. Or 'raspberry' or whatever, doesn't really matter. *Night* doesn't have all that much to do with it . . .

Carly Fine. / I was just making conversation . . .

Greg Great. / Thanks, *Officer* . . .

They wait silently for a moment. Greg glances down at his book, then over at the door – Carly grows more anxious.

Carly Where *is* he?

Greg I dunno. (*Moves towards her.*) Look, Carly, why'd you have to do that? Call Steph and make some big ol' . . .

Carly What? I didn't do anything . . .

Greg Yeah, uh-huh, she's all . . .

Carly I just . . .

Greg You got her totally worked up and, and, and she's completely pissed, and now I can't even get her to take my . . .

Carly I'm sorry, but . . . *she* called me so you're the one with a problem obviously.

Greg What?

Carly She did. On her way to work.

Greg She called *you*?

Carly Yes. *Twice.* / The second time right from the parking lot of Super Cuts . . .

Greg Really? / Why? I mean . . .

Carly Because we're friends, Greg. Because she needed someone to talk to today, and . . .

Greg Yeah, but . . . wait . . .

Carly . . . Because I would never say such a mean and horrible thing to her, *that's* why.

Greg Oh. (*Beat.*) I actually meant the first . . .

Carly So, yeah, she rang me up and we chatted, like friends do. We talked. (*Beat.*) About *you*, mostly.

Greg And – I mean, then, what'd she say? To me?

Carly She didn't say anything to you – it was to *me*, remember? Called me at home.

Greg Right, right, that's what I meant . . .

Carly She said stuff to me. *About* you. Not very nice stuff, either. She talked shit about you, if you really wanna know. OK?

Greg Great.

Carly Yeah, lots of shit and cried a little . . .

Greg Come on . . .

Carly I'm not kidding! (*Beat.*) Said she even put in her *notice*, so . . . there. Happy?

Greg *What*? / Really?

Carly Yep. / I'm not making stuff up to delight and entertain you. Your girlfriend cried on the phone to me and it doesn't matter who called who. It doesn't – she's not mad because her best friend had the . . . *guts* to tell her the truth; she is upset because of the things you've said about her . . .

Greg Thing! *One* thing I said, and it wasn't a, like, some big . . . God damnit, why'd you tell her? Huh? Why?!

Carly Why'd you *say* it?! Right back at you, OK? Why would you ever say a thing like that about someone . . . and particularly a person you supposedly love? (*Beat.*) I'm sorry but nobody, *no*-body, even the most clueless of guys, is gonna make that kind of mistake. You were being honest . . .

Greg No, it wasn't meant to be a – I was saying a loving thing! (*Looks at Carly.*)

Carly *Oh, really* . . .

Greg I was.

Carly Well, I'd send flowers next time instead, maybe . . . 'cause your communication skills *suck*. / The message was lost.

Greg Fine. / Whatever.

Carly Yep. 'Whatever' is right.

Greg Alright, just don't be so . . . don't look so *triumphant* or whatnot. Do not. (*Beat.*) Because you don't know half the . . .

Carly What?

Greg Fuck. Nothing . . .

Carly What?

Greg Forget it. You guys love it when we do crap like this . . .

Carly And what crap is that? Hmm?

Greg You know . . . fuck up.

Carly So you acknowledge it, then?

Greg Of course, yes! I told her that – said I'm sorry for . . . I think I said 'I'm sorry'. I don't remember now. She was yelling . . .

Carly Yeah, she said that . . .

Greg She screamed and was swearing and it got a little . . . you know how she gets. We said stuff. But I think that I, yeah, I'm sure I did. Said 'Forgive me' or something . . .

Carly Well, I'll ask her . . .

Silence for a moment while Carly glances over towards the door, looking for Kent. Greg staring straight at her.

Greg What's that mean?

Carly I'm saying . . . when she calls again I will ask if that's what you did.

Greg So, you mean . . . what? She's not coming home now? This is it? / Is that what you told her to do? Huh?

Carly I dunno. / *No* . . .

Greg Bullshit . . . No, OK, this is bullshit here! Something's going on and it's not just . . . (*To Carly.*) Come on, really. / What's up?

Carly What? / What?

Greg I've never seen her this mad before, I mean, about *any*thing . . . / The fuck's this *really* about? Hmm?! Tell me!

Carly Yeah, well . . . / Hey, don't swear at me, OK?!

Greg No, seriously, Carly, this is, like, a bunch of shit so don't do that to me, alright? Don't get her all . . .

Carly Greg, don't start . . .

Greg Tell me what else you guys said! / Say it! I want you to tell me! / COME ON!

Carly No! Greg, stop it! / Don't! / STOP!

> *Greg goes to grab her by the arm as she gets up but Carly works to shake him off – she has the training, after all – they both freeze as Kent walks in the room.*

Kent Dude. Honey. What's up?

Carly He was . . .

Greg Nothing, man, I just wanted to . . .

Kent Haven't you done enough damage with the ladies lately? Huh?

Greg Kent, I was . . .

Kent Don't start in with my gal, alright? / Getting her all worked up . . . (*Points.*) Respect the belly, dude! The lady is carrying precious cargo . . .

Greg I wasn't . . . / Kent, come on, I'm . . .

Carly It's not anything, Kent, we just . . .

Greg Promise.

Carly Yeah.

Kent Fine. We need to get up there, anyway – got, like, *thirty* pallets of cereal backed up.

Carly Hey, baby . . .

They have a shared moment – a little nuzzle for show. Greg is forced to wait. To watch.

Kent See, that's how you do it, man. Treat 'em nice . . . 'specially the ones with a *badge*.

Carly Yep.

Greg Yeah, great, thanks . . .

Kent Just a tip there, buddy.

Carly Bye, sweetie.

Kent See you at seven, baby. (*Slaps her on the butt.*) Now go keep us *safe*, 'kay?

Another kiss and Carly gathers her items – wanders off and out. Kent watches her go.

Can you imagine if, like, terrorists come in on a mission because they needed crates of Kleenex for their master plan to take over the United States. You think Carly's gonna be of any use in that kind a situation? She carries a set of keys and a flashlight. What's she supposed to do – *smile* 'em to death? Still, amazing ass, you know?

Greg I dunno, man.

Kent You can say it, I don't mind. I'm very OK with it, believe me . . .

Greg Whatever . . . (*Beat.*) And don't try and trick me, dude – you're *totally* jealous of her!

Kent I *know* . . . but I'm talking about in theory here. / Her ass is kicking, right? Come on, just *say* it . . .

Greg Alright. / It's nice, yes.

Kent *Kicking.*

Greg OK, fine! It rocks. (*Beat.*) Jesus . . . don't be such a . . . dick about it . . .

Kent 'S a beautiful thing.

Greg I'm sure . . . too bad her attitude *sucks*.

Kent Ha! Everything else is sweet, too. Whole body, and a great face . . .

Greg OK, OK. (*Beat.*) Anyhow, sorry before, with us getting a little hot there . . .

Kent No worries. I'm totally behind you.

Greg Really?

Kent Hundred per cent. (*Shoves Greg.*) *Totally.*

Greg Yeah, but you were all . . . I mean . . .

Kent Hey, I'm not crazy! Gotta cover my ass, the investment and all. Have to drop on the side of the missus in a flat-out open contest like that, course I do, but I'm completely with you. / (*Beat.*) They're both being cunts about this . . .

Greg Got it. / Thanks. That's . . .

Kent I'm just not willing to make lunch for myself all week so you can feel like some big-time Clarence Darrow – sorry, bro. No can do. / No matter how far back we go . . .

Greg I see. / Fine. OK.

Kent Cool.

Greg Not to be rude, but I've know you since we were *freshmen* – where did you ever hear of Clarence Darrow?

Kent Hey, you're not the only one who reads . . . (*Pulls a magazine out of a pocket in his overalls.*) Ta-da!

Greg Kent, that's a *TV Guide*.

Kent *So?* Plus it's free, dude, in the Sunday paper – how *awesome* is that?

    Kent laughs and fires the magazine on to a nearby counter.

Greg On a scale from one to ten?

    Loud buzzer sounds overhead. Kent slaps Greg on the back, points over at the trophies and pumps his fist as he exits.

(*To himself.*) Pretty fucking awesome.

    Greg sits a moment longer. Head bowed. Finally follows.

A moment with Steph.

Steph Listen, it's weird, I know that, because I don't count looks as my top thing in a guy, not at all – take *Greg*, for instance. He's got a good face, really, not knockout but very OK, yet I never used to even think that to myself, I mean, envision him in that way. Sometimes a friend or, like, a cousin of mine visited a few months back and she whispered to me at a family thing we were at, a barbeque, 'God, he's cute. He's so cute!' And I looked over to where she was pointing, expecting to see a boy from the neighbourhood – we know a lot of people, having grown up here since, like, for ever – and she's pointing to Greg. Just right there, my boyfriend, who's over at the grill and laughing and making burgers for all of us . . . with the sun going down – you know how it shoots a ray out sometimes around something, like a halo, almost – it was doing that and he was bathed in this light for a second, in this splash of gold and creamy light, and I thought, 'Yeah, he is. He really is a handsome man,' but, see, that still isn't a big deal to me. Even though he is good-looking . . . in his own way . . . it's not the thing about him that first made me like him. It isn't.

She thinks about this for a moment, mulling over what she's just said. She nods her head.

I *really* do feel that . . . that I'm *not* this person who gets off on looks or the more, like, physical side of men, *but* when it's the other way around, about *me* . . . it's like, *shit*, you know? (*Laughs.*) 'Meant as a compliment,' he says to me, like that should calm my nerves or something . . . fuck that! I mean, really? My face?! I'm realistic and I know me as a person – I don't have that much going for me, not all educated and smart or anything, and not completely gorgeous, not like some girls out there – but I like what I've got and so I'm gonna protect that. I am. Yeah. (*Beat.*) I mean, wouldn't you?

SCENE THREE

At the mall.
    Greg sitting at a table, waiting. Has a drink in front of him. Checks his watch. A bundle of flowers on the table.
    After a moment, his cell phone rings. He scrambles to get the call before it's gone.

Greg . . . Hello, yes? Hello? Steph? Yeah, it's me. I'm right here. No, down past the Panda Express. (*Beat.*) Hey, hi, I'm so glad that you . . . Hello? No, I'm already *in* the food court. You want me to meet you or . . . No, fine. I'll just wait. 'Bye.

Greg hangs up his cell and waits. Looking around while he does another quick check of his wristwatch. Suddenly, she is there, right in front of him. Steph.
    Greg stands awkwardly. Tries to go for a kiss but ends up bumbling one on her cheek. They sit opposite each other.

Hey. / (*Gives her the bouquet.*) Here . . .

Steph Hey. / (*Takes it.*) Thanks.

Greg Sure. *Thanks* for coming.

Steph 'S OK. I was gonna be in town shopping, anyway. The mall. (*Beat.*) I need scissors.

Greg Oh.

Steph I also have to stop by the apartment and get a few things, too. Is that OK?

Greg Course. Time?

Steph After this . . . do you mind staying out for a while? / Won't take me long.

Greg No, sure, that's . . . / fine.

Steph Good.

Greg I need to sleep at some point, but it's alright if you have to . . . yeah. / Uh-huh.

Steph Cool. / 'Preciate it.

Greg No prob. (*Yawns.*) That's OK . . . I'll just walk around for a bit. Hit the pet store.

They sit quietly for a moment, staring straight ahead. He steals a glance at her, but looks away quickly.

So. So, so, so. (*Beat.*) How'd we get to this place, huh?

Steph Easy.

Greg Yeah?

Steph Yep. You said some stupid shit and this is what happens . . .

Greg Come on, Steph . . .

Steph No, I'm not gonna 'come on' today . . . today is not a 'come on' day. Nope. / It isn't.

27

Greg I'm just saying . . . / OK, fine . . .

Steph What'd you think, I was gonna forget or something?

Greg No, but . . . I mean . . .

Steph Like there'd be some sort of miracle or conversion or what-have-you in a couple days of me being away? I'm not *Jesus* . . .

Greg I know. *God* . . .

Steph Nope. Guess again . . .

Greg Really funny . . .

Steph I don't think so. I don't think this is one bit funny, Greg, and I hope you can see that.

Greg I do, I get that. I'm sorry, but I'm . . . I'm . . .

Steph What? What're you, confused?

Greg Yeah, I am. I am a lot.

Steph Well, don't be, OK, you shouldn't be. It is not that confusing – you opened my eyes to a lot of shit, that's all. My life.

Greg I'm . . . by what? By me saying that one . . . ?

Steph Yes. *That.*

Greg But come on, I didn't . . . Stephanie, let's be serious here. Alright? Let's. (*Beat.*) I said one thing. Alright? A *stupid* little thing . . . / I know.

Steph Yeah, about *me*. / I mean, I can take a lot, pretty much, anyway, but I'm, like, my face? That's shit. It just is . . . (*Beat.*) And even if I was, ugly, I'm saying, even if I was not cute, unattractive by world standards, don't I wanna be with someone who finds me beautiful? I think so. It's not like a math equation or anything, Greg, it is fairly simple. I can't be with a guy who finds me unpleasant to look at.

Greg I don't!

Steph Let's not get into it again, OK, because I'm not gonna be able to deal . . . / *What*? / Fuck that, I don't know anybody here.

Greg OK, OK . . . Shhh . . . / Do you have to be so, like . . . *loud* all the time? / Fine.

She shakes her head, putting an end to that part of the chat. He opens his mouth to say something else but stops.
She glances at her watch and checks her phone. He watches her, shaking his head but saying nothing.

So, you wanna get a bite or something? / Salad?

Steph No thanks. / *No.*

Greg Come on . . . it's lunchtime, isn't it? It's time to eat and you're, you know, racing around town or whatever, you're not gonna stop and eat, plus the drive back – You're staying with your folks, right?

Steph Yes. I'm . . . yeah. Until I find a place.

Greg So, OK, then. Why don't we just . . . ?

Steph Don't, alright? Don't try to act like it didn't happen and I'm just having a 'girl thing' here because that's not the story, *bud*. It is not. (*Beat*.) We can't eat lunch and kiss each other and start blabbing on the phone next week . . . We're done, Greg. I am finished with our relationship and I'm gonna need you to acknowledge that before I go . . . (*Pointing*.) Flowers don't save the day.

Greg Stephanie, this is crazy, all the stuff you're saying because I really care for you and you do, too, I know you do . . .

Steph No! That's not true. Don't speak for me. (*Beat*.)

You always wanna say shit for me, vouch for me or sign shit that we should both have our names on and I'm not gonna have it any more . . . You are not me, so you don't know. (*Sits forward.*) Listen to me very carefully, OK, 'cause I'm only gonna say this the one time. Fuck off . . . that's what I want you to do, Greg, get the fuck out of my life and leave me alone, let me start over in a serious fashion, maybe in a relationship or not, I dunno, but if it is in something like that, may it please, *please* be with someone who can keep from being an asshole and thinking they know everything, because you don't. You do not know a goddamn thing to do with me is what I've discovered in my four years with you. Four years that are now gone . . . so totally lost and gone that it makes me cry when I see any little bit from our time together. A key ring or, or your name light up on my phone or . . . shit. (*She starts crying.*) Fuck, fuck, fuck.

> Greg tries to scoot closer and comfort her but she pulls away like he's holding a branding iron.

STOP. Why would you . . . ? God. Idiot.

Greg . . . I'm trying to comfort you . . .

Steph Yeah, well, don't.

Greg I was just . . . / *Jeez* . . .

Steph NO. / No more . . . (*Beat.*) Look, I'm gonna need your keys.

Greg . . . Great.

Steph *What*?

Greg Nothing.

Steph No, what? I left mine in my other purse.

Greg Fine.

Steph OK then. Fuck. It's a *key*, Greg, I didn't ask for half your pay cheque or something.

Greg (*to himself*) Yeah, well, you couldn't . . .

Steph What's that?

Greg Forget it.

Steph No, I wanna hear what you said.

Greg (*digs in pocket*) Here's my key . . . I'll get it off the . . . Lemme . . . Shit, I don't have any nails, can you do it?

He hands over the keys and she proceeds to remove the key from the rest of the set.

Steph Thanks. / I'll leave it under the mat.

Greg Yup. / Super.

Steph And your car, too. I'm gonna pick mine up while I'm there, so we don't have to . . . / Sorry I took it but I was pissed. I mean, obviously.

Greg Cool. / Do what you gotta do.

Steph Ohhh, you're all Mr Casual now, is that it?

Greg Whatever.

Steph You're such a dick.

Greg How do you want me to act, Steph? Huh? I am trying to be nice here, to, to, to . . . make up with you or kiss your ass, which is what I figured you were after – getting on my *knees* practically to make it up to you but no – you've gotta keep pushing it, pushing me away by saying that we're done – what the hell is all that crap? You're so angry . . . none of this makes any sense, and I just wanna go home. Ya know? Just go back to the house and climb into bed with you, say 'I'm sorry' again if you want me to, but crawl in and have you up against me . . . your back against me and I can feel your heartbeat when we get all quiet like that . . . that's what I want.

Steph Oh. / I see.

Greg That's what I'd like. / Yeah.

Steph So, you wanna feel my back, be there up against me that way . . .

Greg Yes . . .

Steph Why, so you don't gotta look at my face?

Greg Oh, God! FUCK!! / You're crazy! You really are!!

Steph Hey, *you* said it . . . / It's you saying it, you're the one!

Greg I'm trying to make up with you! / I *am*!

Steph Then say something *nice*, try that! / No, you're not!

Greg Yes! / I am, too! / *And* flowers . . .

Steph No! / No, uh-uh, you're not . . . / Ohhh, big fucking deal . . .

Greg I do not get you, I really don't . . .

Steph That's because you don't try!

Greg Bullshit!

Steph BULLSHIT!

She throws the keys back at him, hitting him hard. They bounce off and scatter on the floor.

Greg Oww, damnit! (*Beat.*) . . . Fine.

Steph Yeah.

Greg Do what you want.

Steph I am. Done it.

Greg Good, then get the hell outta here . . .

Steph I will.

Greg . . . You and your, your . . . *stupid* face.

She turns on him, almost spitting out the next bit as she gets to her feet.

Steph I knew it! / I KNEW YOU HATED ME! You fucking asshole!

Greg Joke! / I was joking!

Steph Fuck jokes! That's not a joke, what you said about me is no joke, asshole, and you know it . . . / You KNOW that!

Greg Take it easy . . . / I was *kidding* . . . Jesus, can't even make a little . . .

Steph I'm not gonna take it easy, who the fuck are these people, I couldn't care less!!

Greg Steph, stop it, now . . . / Stop . . .

Steph Shut up! / Shut your big sideways-grinning mouth, that's what I want you to do. OK?! (*Beat.*) Keep your damn mouth closed for a minute and listen to me . . .

She scrambles into her purse, looking for something. Greg looks around, embarrassed by what's happening.

Greg We should probably just . . . / Go. Now.

Steph NO! / Sit.

She digs a bit more and comes up with a piece of paper.

Here. This. This is what I wanted. Here. (*Opening it.*) I've made this over the last however long . . . I dunno, since I left, and it covers all your shit. All the crap I'm feeling about you but have held my tongue on . . . I was gonna email you, but this here is way better. (*Looks around.*) People! Hey you guys over there, check this out . . . / I want you all to hear this, this is good.

Greg Stephanie, don't. / Fucking hell, man . . . (*Reaching for her.*) Why do you have to be so . . . *Please* . . .

Steph Sit down, Greg, and *listen* for once. / This might help you with your next girlfriend.

Greg Why? / Seriously, Steph, why are you . . . ?

Steph (*reading*) 'Greg, your hair is thinning – I'm a hairdresser so I should know. You try and hide it pretty well but I can spot it, at the crown when you're bending over or as you sit in the kitchen eating and you ask me to get up and fix you something, then I see it. Two years, that's what I give it. And in front, too, but that may hold . . .'

Greg For fuck's sake . . .

Steph 'I don't like your eyes. I never have. I think they're small and piggish and you make it worse by squinting a lot. If you ever wore the sunglasses I bought you at Christmas – they were fucking *expensive* – it would help but you don't so your eyes look like shit and you're starting to get wrinkles there, too. Your nose. Where do I begin with your nose? It's your mom's so I should be kind, but hey . . . fuck that. Your nostrils make me sick and I always have to look up into them because we have the most *un*imaginative sex that a person could ever come up with . . . I think you're gay, maybe – Seriously, you should check into that because you sure have trouble doing it with me and I'm fine. I know I like it, even with you, so I'm guessing it's you. Your teeth are OK – just – but I don't like your lips at all. Your mouth is wide and

34

your lips are way too thick to be sexy and I hate kissing you. This is a shame but it's true, I've hated kissing you from almost the first time we did it and that's really depressing. Your tongue is like this little poker and you move it too fast and . . . well, you get the idea. It sucks.' (*To him.*) Greg. Are you listening?

Greg . . . Yep. I am. (*Beat.*) Yes.

Greg starts to say something else but catches himself. He remains seated. Steph seems satisfied and continues.

Steph Good. (*Reads.*) 'I've never thought you had a great body, it's OK, but nothing really special and I hate how you walk around – not just at home but outside during the summer or at the gym; a lot, anyway – like you are super cute or something, like you have all these muscles and a nice stomach or whatever. You don't. You never have, so stop doing that. It's kind of pathetic; I am not the only person who thinks that . . . I'm not gonna be so crass as to say much about your dick because that would put me on your level – being hurtful – but I will say this: you're way too hairy down there and most girls find that disgusting. Your balls, too, it kind of makes me gag when I go there. I guess there's nothing you can really do about that – guys don't wax or anything like we do – but you should be aware of it, anyway. It's gross. Enough said. Your legs are fine, probably one of your best features . . . Your feet are the worst, though. They are. Your toes are, they're like, almost like fingers *and* you bite your own toenails – I know you do, I've seen you – and that goes down as the most disgusting fact I know. The fact that you rip off your toe nails with your teeth . . . and then eat them, or nibble at them, anyway, after you've done it. And sometimes you smell. A little . . . You do because you think that you don't have to shower after work and you'll get in bed and sleep and sweat some more and then

35

use a little deodorant and off you go, like, to work or wherever. And so you stink, kind of, but I've stopped speaking about it to you because you don't listen. You do not fucking listen.' / (*Waiting.*) I guess that would be it . . .

Steph crumples the paper into a ball and drops it on the table – grabs up the keys and gets ready to go.

Greg *Wow.* / You . . . you did that to hurt me.

Steph No shit.

Greg You don't really feel all that stuff.

Steph No?

Greg You couldn't . . .

Steph Really?

Greg No. I mean, I don't think so. I don't see how you could and, and still – I mean, it just isn't possible to feel that kind of, like, hatred – I guess that's what it is – and still want to be with a person.

Steph Love is blind, shithead. It is.

Greg Yeah, but . . .

Steph I could feel all that and *still* love you. It's possible.

Greg Stephanie . . .

Steph Until somebody had to go and open his big fucking mouth. (*To the others.*) OK, show's over now, go back to your chop suey shit that you're eating and leave us be . . .

Steph watches the crowd disperse; turns to Greg again.

Greg This shouldn't be happening . . .

Steph But it is.

Greg I care about you, Stephanie. I honestly do.

Steph You just don't get it . . .

Greg No, I really don't. No. (*Beat.*) It is the same thing you just said to me – I get why you did it like that so you could teach a lesson, fine – but it's the same thing I did.

Steph It's not.

Greg And why's that? Huh? Please, just explain that one bit to me and then you can go.

Steph Because, Greg . . .

Greg (*smiles*) And I like your face, I do . . . I've always thought you were . . . it's gonna sound stupid now, but you know I have. It is a really, really . . . cute face. / You're cute, Steph. You are. Adorable.

Steph Yeah? / *Thanks.*

Greg Of course. (*Beat.*) So why's it different? Seriously, I don't get it.

Steph I know you don't.

Greg But how come? *Why?*

Steph Because this stuff, all this stuff I said about you? (*Holds up list.*) Right here?

Greg Yeah?

Steph . . . I made most of it up. To hurt you. (*Beat.*) I wrote it down and I read it out loud but it's not true. I mean, it is, some of it, but I embellished it. But what you said about me – even though it's just that one thing – it is completely and for all time's sake true. You meant it.

Greg . . . Stephanie . . .

Steph And *that* is why. (*She crumples up the page and drops it.*) I'm taking the bedroom TV. I bought it with my own money and so I'm taking it.

With that she turns and exits, disappearing off down the hall. Shoes clacking on the tiles. Leaves the flowers.
    Greg looks around, then carefully opens the paper ball on the table. Flattens it out. Begins reading.

SCENE FOUR

At work.
    Carly and Kent seated at a table, eating. Carly watches as Kent keeps checking the time.

Carly . . . You're not late.

Kent 'Kay.

Carly I don't know why you have to keep looking at your watch.

Kent *Because* . . . we've got a lot to do tonight.

Carly Oh.

Kent Putting in overtime, might as well do the thing right. Make a good job of it or at least give it my best. You know?

Carly Wow. Listen to you . . .

Kent I'm just sayin', baby. / We don't all get to *Barney Fife* our way through life.

Carly Fine. / Yeah, yeah . . .

Kent I don't like doing a shoddy job, is all. If I do then somebody notices and I'm not the guy they call for the extra shifts or the holiday hours or that type of deal . . . and you know you like the money.

Carly Everybody likes money.

Kent Uh-uh. / That's not true.

Carly Who? / Who that you know doesn't like some money?

Kent I'm only making a point here . . .

Carly Then make it.

Kent I *am*. You like clothes and stuff so you can cook and fix up the nursery and shit like that, right? Oodles of items that we order with our pay cheques off QVC, so I don't get why you're busting my balls when I say that I'm trying to be a useful member of my team tonight which can only lead to more work which equals money and additional crap to purchase and wear and eat. / OK?

Carly Fine. / God . . .

Kent That's all I'm saying.

Carly Great. Point, set and . . . whatever.

Kent Match. If you're meaning tennis.

Carly . . . Yes. 'Match.' You win.

Kent Wasn't trying to *win* anything. Just . . .

Carly Can we drop it now?

Kent Course.

Carly Good.

Kent It's dropped. (*Mimes a drop.*) Plop! Plop!

He pokes her in the rib. She jumps up and pushes him away.

Carly Don't! God, you're so . . . ten. That's what you are, you're like a ten-year-old. I'm living with some dude who's a child and thinks that because he works an extra shift he can just be a . . . a . . . *infant* about the rest of his life.

39

Kent . . . Mommy . . . gimme milk, *Mommy* . . .

He half rises, reaching out for her, pawing her breasts. She recoils and then moves away. Angry now.

Carly Stupid . . .

Kent I'm . . . I don't have to go yet. We can sit here for a while if you like. (*Grins.*) You can even *cuff* me if you wanna . . .

Carly No, I'm tired of you now.

Kent That's nice.

Carly I am.

Kent Well, damn, baby, I don't know what sort of remedy I've got for that . . .

Carly I do. I've got a remedy, which is to take off and go to my station. That way, I don't even have to see you . . .

Kent Fuck! I'm sorry that I wanted to start early or whatever . . . Damn. (*Beat.*) Rich's got his eye on me lately – finally took it off *you* for a second, don't think I missed that – now he's watching me, so I'm, you know . . .

Carly Doesn't matter.

Kent Yeah, it does. It totally matters. Let's not pretend, OK, 'cause he's being pretty obvious about it . . . (*Beat.*) Sorry that I'm watching the time, it's got absolutely no bearing on whether I wanted to see you or not – because I do – but I'm also trying to be a useful employee which can only be of benefit to our lifestyle and that, I'm seeing now, places me in a bit of a bind. (*Beat.*) Puts a fucking *crimp* in my plans.

Carly Yep.

Kent Well, I'd never pick work over you so I'm sorry that you ever thought that was the case . . . I'm here to tell you that it's not and I'm happy to hang out till Rich comes looking for me with your other pals from security . . .

Carly Yeah? / Hmm . . .

Kent Yes. / (*Smiles.*) Better?

Carly . . . A little.

She smiles. They go to it – kissing and carrying on. Greg wanders through the doors and they stop immediately. Carly looks at him, turns to Kent, kisses him and crosses out – not a word to Greg.

Greg . . . Well, hey, that's good. Everything's back to normal, I see.

Kent Gotta give 'er time, dude.

Greg Right. (*Yawns.*) Shit!

Kent Steph's her best friend. / She's basically holding you responsible for her closest pal moving away and all that, so give 'er a little space, alright?

Greg Fine. / She can . . . God, I was coming to get some coffee, you know? / Didn't mean to create some *international* thing here.

Kent It's cool. / Sit down.

Greg Thanks. (*Takes out a book.*) Anyway . . .

Kent She was mad at me before, so I'm sure it just carried over. / What're you reading?

Greg Oh. / Hawthorne. / Early American stuff. Kinda like Gothic. Allegories.

Kent Huh. / (*Grabs it.*) 'The Birth Mark.' O-*kay*. Anyway . . . she's just lashing out for no reason – well, not 'no' reason, but barely.

Greg Women, huh?

Kent Yep. (*Hands back the book.*) No shit.

Greg That pretty much says it all . . .

Kent Oh yeah.

Greg One day they're gonna save a little time and just stick that in the dictionary. Just the word, no definition necessary, and any guy who stumbles across it'll just roll his eyes and know what the hell it means. (*Beat.*) 'Women.'

Kent Totally.

Greg I'm so . . . you know. Over it.

Kent What?

Greg Them. Her. (*Starts to drink.*) Damn . . .

Kent Right. (*Beat.*) Get your car back yet?

Greg Uh-huh. / 'Bout, I dunno, two weeks ago . . .

Kent Nice. / She bang it up or anything? That's a typical trick, after they get mad and all that – ding up the paint or smack the fender into something.

Greg Shit . . . You know I never even checked?

Kent You better.

Greg Yeah.

Kent I could absolutely see her doing that . . . after what you said. (*Beat.*) No offence, but she can be a twat sometimes, dude. Even back at school that was true . . .

Greg . . . I didn't even think to . . .

Kent I'm just *saying*. / After how she took it.

Greg . . . Sure. / Right.

Kent rises, checks his watch.

42

Kent (*to himself*) . . . Come on, come on.

Greg What's up?

Kent Huh? Oh, nothing . . .

Greg No, seriously. What?

Kent Nothing, man, don't worry about it.

Greg Just asking.

Kent I'm hanging, that's all.

Greg Cool. / No prob.

Kent Exactly. / Heard who we're playing – it's that fucking bail-bonds team! Pricks.

Greg *Great* . . . (*Beat.*) Dude, you seem anxious. Sure you're OK?

Kent Yeah, I'm just . . . yep, yep, yep.

Greg What?

Kent I dunno. Waiting.

Greg I see. (*Smiles.*) Very cryptic, my friend.

Kent That's 'cause you're . . . Don't worry about it.

Greg What? Now what am I?

Kent You know what you are . . .

Greg No, I don't, I don't know what the hell you're talking about here – acting all goofy since I walked in tonight.

Kent Dude, you're *way* too chatty at work, if you want the details so damn bad . . .

Greg *What?!*

Kent Don't feel like I can trust you . . . (*Beat.*) Maybe I'm paranoid, but I don't think so.

43

Greg You're fucking nuts, man, because . . . if anybody has issues with privacy it's your *wife*, OK? / Let's be honest here.

Kent Fine. / That's true . . . Carly's the worst with a secret! Fucking *bigmouth*.

Greg And I don't even get what you're going on about . . . What'm I privy to about you? *You* have issues, that's what's going on here.

Kent Maybe. (*Beat.*) Mouth shut, OK?

Greg Promise.

Kent It's Crystal.

Greg What is?

Kent (*smiles*) The new girl, up in the shipping department. (*Digs out his phone to find a cell picture he took.*) You *know*.

Greg Who? / (*Glances at screen.*) I can't see . . .

Kent Her. / *Look*. The chick with the face.

Greg Oh yeah, right, right – I had no idea what her name was. So what about her?

Kent I'm, you know . . . (*Waits.*) *Duh* . . .

Greg No.

Kent I've been seeing her. Lately.

Greg What're you . . . what's that mean? You're . . . you are?

Kent Uh-huh.

Greg *Really*?

Kent Month or so. / Little over.

Greg Yeah? / You're kidding me.

Kent No. Why would I?

Greg Ahhh, to sound cool, maybe. Or to yank my chain, like usual . . .

Kent Yeah, well, not this time. (*Beat.*) 'S been a ball, lemme tell you. I mean, you think she looks good in those dress clothes, you should see her in a pair a' shorts. *Fuck*, man . . . / Her legs're like those girls who play soccer, ya know? But not all muscly and shit . . . just very shapely. *solid*.

Greg Great. / That's *super*, Kent.

Kent Hey, don't judge. It's just a thing, it happened, I can't help it.

Greg No, I'm sure . . . probably didn't have much to do with it, really. Right?

Kent Actually, no. Few smiles, 'How's tricks?' and that was about it. / Came to one of our games and asked me out for a drink. I said 'OK' and there you go . . .

Greg God . . . / And she knows about Carly?

Kent Fuck yeah. Whole deal is square with her, why I don't know. Some girls like that . . . the whole competition thing. (*Beat.*) Maybe she looks at her and thinks, 'This dude *must* be worth it, a woman like that on his arm.' I dunno, I'm not Nostradamus.

Greg Yeah, good, thanks for clearing that up, 'cause I was pretty confused . . .

Kent I'm just *saying* – she gets it, she's aware and there's no problem. (*Beat.*) And she is fine, man, lemme tell you. Twenty-three, so, you know, only starting to fade a bit.

Greg . . . You're disgusting . . .

Kent *What?!* She's amazing, she is, it's just not, like a, you know . . . some teenager or whatever. Their skin is – I'm not being a perv or anything – but . . .

Greg Thank *God* for that . . .

Kent It's just a fact! Amazing to the touch is all, some, you know . . . a gymnast or one of those cheerleaders, that age. *Tight.*

Greg Alright, that's it . . . (*Stands.*) I'm gonna head out now. Look, if you like her so much then, you know, so be it. Go for it.

Kent Thanks. / And dude . . .

Greg Sure. / What?

Kent I'm serious here. Not a word, OK?

Greg I won't. / Promise.

Kent To *any*body. / Not Stephanie, no one.

Greg Really funny.

Kent I'm just saying – if you make up or, or, you know . . . whatever. Can't mention it.

Greg I don't think that's happening, but fine.

Kent *Or* to the guys down at your end there . . . I don't need Rich or those assholes hearing about it. / Want it on the down low.

Greg Kent, take it easy, alright? / 'S none of my business, do what you need to do . . .

Kent I will.

Greg That's your stuff. I've got my own shit to deal with . . .

Kent No kidding.

Greg What's that mean?

Kent *Means* your back axle could be all knocked out've alignment and you don't even know it yet . . . (*Smiles.*) *Chicks*, right?

Greg Yeah. Pretty damn lethal. (*Beat.*) And so you and Carly, you guys are, like . . . what?

Kent No problems. / We're perfect.

Greg Right. / *Uh-huh.*

Kent Seriously! This new thing just, you know, makes it *more* than perfect . . . (*Beat.*) She is a knockout, she really is. Crystal. / Her face is, like . . . ummmgh! Fuck.

Greg Uh-huh. / I don't doubt it.

Kent Don't need to, I'm telling you she is and she is. (*Smiles.*) *And* she's got roommates.

A loud buzzer sounds.

Greg Great. (*Beat.*) I'm gonna get going.

Kent What . . . You don't have time to hear this now? / How I'm feeling about her?

Greg No, what? / No, go ahead, I'm just – go on. Say what you're gonna say.

Kent I'm telling you . . . when you get up close to her – Crystal, I'm saying – she's got the most awesome features. I'm serious. These teeth that're . . . and her lips. Find myself just staring at 'em sometimes, and her eyes are a colour, I don't even think it's one you'd find in a box of crayons – maybe one of those bigger cartons, like, sixty-four colours, with the sharpener in it – but even then I'm not sure. They're kinda green, but sorta blue, too. Almost hypnotic. (*Smiles.*) Listen to me! Like a fucking kid. / That's what she does to me.

Greg 'S great. / No, that's great, Kent.

Kent It's whatever, man, but it's smacked me for a loop, tell you that much. Anyway, I'll see you later.

Kent exits.
Greg tries to read, but it's no use. He sees that Kent's left his garbage – he scoops all of it up and carries it over to the bin. Drops it in. Another loud buzzer sounds. Kent appears at the door to the break room.

Kent Dude. Second buzzer. What the fuck! You wanna get written up?

Greg I'm coming.

Kent Good. And remember –

Greg What? / Got it.

Kent – keep this shit to yourself. / You know I'd do the same for you . . . totally would. And us guys gotta stick together, right?

Greg Right.

Kent We're like fucking buffaloes out here!

Greg Yeah.

Kent exits, a punch to Greg's arm as he goes off.

. . . and look what happened to them.

Greg exits.

A moment with Kent.

Kent . . . it's interesting, having a wife who looks the way mine does. Attractive, I'm saying. It really is. It's probably not what you'd think it'd be, all great

and wonderful at every turn of the road; it has its
disadvantages, believe you me. Seriously. (*Beat.*) I mean,
it's nice as well, I don't mean to imply it's not . . . You
enjoy her, you're knocked out by her as this lady that you
feel the . . . *need* to possess or have as your own, but in
the end, I mean, from that day on – once you *do* get her –
you start to worry about keeping her because of all these
other guys who're having the same damn fantasy about
'er that you did! So you got that, there's that fear to
contend with, plus I gotta deal with all the crap I get
from people about her being a *detective* or whatever,
wearing a uniform and all that shit – it's humiliating,
really, even having her at my place of work, but we're
stuck needing two incomes. Now what with the fucking
kid coming. She was gonna just be on the line at one
point, that's what she first came in and applied for, but
then they had an opening in security and one of these
big cheeses out front – this dumbshit over in human
resources – says he'd like to help her out and suggests an
easier job, up near him where she can sit and watch all
the video cameras, sign vendors in and out at the door –
plus, he says, 'You make a really great first impression
for our company.' How fucking lame's that, how bad he
wants to take a shot at her? The prick. (*Beat.*) I don't
mind so much, I guess, but she's always in the halls or
down on the floor, strutting around and I hate having to
watch myself so much, who I'm talking to or whatever . . .
Pain in the ass. Can't believe sometimes that this is the
life that God's staked out for me in his *infinite* plan –
then I think, who'm I kidding?! He hasn't got any 'plan'!
I've got a job in some warehouse and a limited number
of skills and a Chevrolet that I'd like to take a blowtorch
to . . . That's my life in the foreseeable future. (*Smiles.*)
Look, don't listen to me, I'm doing OK, I'm just being
silly. In fact, I've got a little something interesting that
has flared up here as of late and I'm gonna just . . . see

where the day takes me – which is what most guys do, right? We ride that wave. Yep. Ride it to shore and see what comes of it. Hey, that's how it's done – 'S the way we get by. It pretty much is.

End of Act One.

Act Two

SCENE ONE

At a restaurant.
  Greg stands, waiting in the lobby. Checks his watch once or twice, watching the door. After a moment, Steph walks past.
  They see each other and stop cold. Silence for a moment.

Greg . . . Steph.

Steph Oh. Hi.

Greg Hey.

Steph Wow. I'm . . .

Greg Surprise.

  Steph nods her head, unsure what to do next. Greg waits.

Steph Huh. So, this is . . . you know. Funny.

Greg Yep.

Steph Seeing you here.

Greg Right.

Steph Yeah, it's . . . umm . . . I'm working over at a salon nearby, so that's . . . but yeah.

Greg What're you . . . So, are you, like, in there having dinner or something? / A meal?

Steph Uh-huh. / Dinner.

Greg 'Kay.

Steph Yep. You?

Greg Waiting. (*Points.*) We had a double-header tonight, so . . . that's why I'm dressed like this. / Casual male. Attire.

Steph Ahhh. / Cool.

Greg Umm-hmm. (*Beat.*) And are you . . . you know?

Steph What?

Greg You *know*. With your new *salon* buddies?

Steph No.

Greg OK. Not your parents, though. I mean, that'd be kinda weird – not *weird*, but – on a, like, Wednesday night. So . . .

Steph No.

Greg Carly?

Steph Nope, not anybody you know . . .

Greg I see. Good. (*Backtracks.*) I just mean . . . you know, wouldn't wanna see anybody that we're both friends with. / Or . . .

Steph Uh-huh. / And you? Who're you waiting for?

Greg Just . . . people. / From work.

Steph Oh. / I see. Not a girl?

Greg . . . No.

Steph Me either. (*Grins.*) I mean, I'm not with a girl, either. / So . . .

Greg 'Kay. / Although that would explain a *lot*.

Steph Ha-ha. (*Beat.*) It's just dinner.

Greg Fine.

Steph Yes, it is. It's a very fine and nice time that I'm having. It's a great place.

Greg I like it, too . . . I mean, the *lobby*.

Steph I don't know why we never came here as a couple. Back then, I'm saying.

Greg No, yeah, I get what you mean. I'm not sure, actually . . . little bit out of town, I suppose.

Steph That might be it.

Greg 'Cause we did like to eat out, didn't we? I mean, back in the . . . *yesteryear*.

Steph We did, yes.

Greg All kinds of spots.

Steph Mmm.

Greg That's . . . remember that crazy little, what do they call it, *fondue* restaurant? With all the cheese sauces and crap like that?

Steph Which, with the . . . ? / Oh, sure. Right.

Greg Yeah. That one. / Had that Alpine-looking roof on it and everybody running around in, whatever-they callems? *Lederhosen* or something like that . . . 'The Cheddar Hut. Welcome to the Cheddar Hut!'

Steph Exactly! (*Laughs.*) That was funny . . .

Greg Yep. Good eats, though.

Steph True.

Greg I mean, for all the silliness.

Steph Right . . .

They stand for a moment, nodding. Unsure what else to say to each other. Greg checks the time.

Greg If you need to go, you should . . .

Steph Yeah, probably. Just going to the ladies room, don't wanna appear like I took off or anything . . .

Greg No.

Steph Not a good first impression.

Greg Oh . . . So, I mean . . . this is, like, a first date or something?

Steph Yep. Well, I've actually known him for a while, but – doesn't matter. / Yes.

Greg I see. / That's . . . huh. Huh-huh-huh.

Steph What?

Greg Nothing. (*Smiles.*) Good for you.

Steph I'll bet . . .

Greg No, seriously. Congrats.

Steph You're not wishing me 'good luck', Greg, I know you. You're wishing the guy gets a bone stuck in his throat or something . . .

Greg Yeah, but I hope *you* have a good time. (*Beat.*) And you can always kill his pets if you don't.

Steph Ha! (*Laughs.*) Whatever . . .

Greg Uh-huh. What-ever.

Steph That's . . . I mean, I know we went through a bit of shit there recently, a few crappy months or whatnot, but it doesn't hurt to wish another person well, really doesn't.

Greg OK.

Steph 'OK' what? Why do you always answer me or other people with something so . . . God, so fucking abstruse in response to what we say to you? Why do you do that?

Greg Steph, you know what? I don't even know a word that could *describe* that word . . . let alone what that one means, so I doubt I'm being that. Whatever it is. (*Beat.*) And ya know what? I read a *lot*, so . . . that's . . .

Steph No, but *I'm* trying to make a life for myself, OK? Trying to grow and, and . . . shit. Nothing.

Greg Good, go for it. Knock yourself out.

Steph And it's just, like . . . impossible for you to wish me happiness, right? To hope that I might have that happen to me?

Greg You know what, it might be a little early to ask me to perform 'big-hearted', OK? (*Beat.*) You're at a good restaurant, I can only imagine that you're with some decent guy who's gonna treat you well and drives a nice car and thinks you're the fucking apple of his eye – don't be surprised when he tries to get in your panties if you go for anything more than the ziti, but – I'll bet he's amazing and I hope he is the height of *passion* and all that . . . Stephanie, I wish you only the best. I'm serious when I say this: have a beautiful life. Now can you go back in there and just let me wait for my friends? Huh?

Steph (*to herself*) . . . You're such a prick.

Greg That's even classier when you're wearing a dress. / 'S nice.

Steph Fuck you. / I'm trying to look pretty, alright?! I'm *trying* to make myself feel better because my former boyfriend – this guy that I gave a whole lot of my heart to – couldn't find me attractive and left me wondering what's wrong with me. Why I was so unappealing to him . . . (*Beat.*) So, yeah, I'm wearing a *skirt* tonight so that I feel a little sexier, or cuter or, you know . . . what the *hell* do you care?

Greg I don't. I'm not at all worried about it.

Steph Bullshit . . .

Greg Bull-shit.

Steph I see you looking at me – even now I can see you glancing down at my legs and all that crap . . . you totally miss me. My body.

Greg Wow . . . you're going for the mother lode tonight, huh?

Steph The fuck's that mean?

Greg You want this new guy *and* me, 's that it? / Approval from the whole damn group . . .

Steph No . . . / That's not what I'm . . .

Greg Well, you know what, fine, I'll toss you a bone, makes you feel any better – I just can't *live* with myself knowing that I've made you feel bad . . . (*Smirks.*) Listen, you look wonderful, yes, you do, but so what? You never wore that get-up with me, so it doesn't exactly thrill me to tell you all that, build you up about your dress . . .

Steph It's new. And it's a *skirt*, not a dress.

Greg Whatever! Bought for tonight, I suppose.

Steph Yes.

Greg That's great.

Steph I had to have something.

Greg Sure.

Steph You'd do the same thing . . .

Greg Yeah? Really? Look at me, you recognise anything I've got on?

Steph Of course . . .

Greg Well, then, I guess your little theory there is full of shit . . .

Steph What's that mean?

Greg Nothing. / Just forget it . . .

Steph No, what? / . . . So you are meeting someone then, is that what you're saying?

Greg doesn't respond immediately – he glances at his watch again while Steph looks over her shoulder, back into the restaurant.

Greg No. Maybe. / Yes.

Steph I see. / Is it that *new* girl?

Greg No! I've never even met her before.

Steph But it's a date.

Greg It's a *meeting*. Some friends are just, you know . . . introducing us.

Steph Sure.

Greg It's more of a gathering, really. / That's all. At the bar . . .

Steph Oh. / *Here?*

Greg Not my idea.

Steph That's terrific . . .

Greg It's whatever. (*Beat.*) Least I didn't get all dressed up for it . . .

Steph Well, that just makes you a slob, then, doesn't it?

Greg . . . And so what does that make you?

Without thinking Steph reaches over and slaps Greg across the face. He doesn't react. She glances around, feeling a bit ashamed.

Steph Fuck . . . I'm sorry.

Greg That's alright. I'm sure they can wire it shut and I can still have the *soup* . . .

Steph Seriously, are you OK?

Greg I'm fine.

Steph Lemme see . . . (*Tries to look.*) Here . . .

Greg No.

Steph Greg, let me . . .

Greg Stop it.

Steph I didn't mean to do it, I just . . .

Greg Stephanie, drop it! For once just shut up and fucking let it go . . . (*Beat.*) You can't just turn it off and on, alright, however you're feeling about a person. You can't.

Steph I'm not, I'm . . . / (*Reaches out.*) Please.

Greg NO. / *Don't.* You can walk out on me for . . . some *perceived* slight that I did you, some horrible judgement I made about your womanhood, you can swear at me and, and, hit me – whatever the hell suits you – you just go ahead and do, that's always been the way with you – but you're not gonna be able to make up with me any time you want or look at my cheek right now or call me when this miserable shithead that you're out with tonight hurts you, because he is gonna, he will, he's a guy and so it's a done deal . . . he will find a way to damage you and that's

58

a fact. But you know what? I will not be there for you. I won't be. (*Beat.*) You will be on your own then and you're gonna realise I wasn't so bad . . .

Steph I'll . . . I'm going back to dinner now.

Greg You do that.

Steph We're almost done, so I'll . . .

Greg No, don't worry about it.

Steph I'm *not* staying.

Greg Please don't make a scene, OK? Just be a little mature here . . . if that's not too . . .

Steph Yeah, so what do you suggest, then, huh?

Greg Simple. I'm gonna wait here – hopefully a doctor will come along and be able to reset my jaw – then I'm gonna nab my friends as they arrive and we'll go to some other place.

Steph Oh.

Greg So . . .

Steph You'd do that?

Greg Of course. 'S just a bar, right? / They got Budweiser all over town, so . . .

Steph Yeah, but . . . / that's . . .

Greg I don't wanna run the risk of you hitting my date or anything. / Don't even know her *name* yet . . .

Steph Right. / (*Smiles.*) Thanks . . .

Greg No prob.

Steph OK, so . . . Then . . . (*Thinking.*) Wow, that's really kind of unexpected from you, so thank you. I'm surprised, I guess. Yeah. I just think that's really nice, so . . .

Greg Yeah. I'll see you some time . . . oh, and remind the new guy to add 9-1-1 to his speed dial. Might save his life.

Steph Ha-ha.

Greg Have fun.

Steph *Sure.*

Greg No, honestly. Do. (*Beat.*) Bet he drives a . . . convertible, right? / Hmm?

Steph You suck. / Yes.

Greg It's a gift.

Steph *Anyways* . . .

Greg Ha! So long.

Steph You, too. Enjoy yourself, I guess . . .

Greg I don't know how anything can surpass the fun I've already had, but . . .

Steph You're such a dick . . . (*Smiles.*) 'Bye.

> *Steph starts off – she is almost gone when Greg calls out to her.*

Greg Steph? (*Waits for her to turn.*) You really do look great in your little outfit there. With all that . . . whatever the hell it is.

Steph I dunno. It's called 'asymmetrical'. / The way it's cut like that, I mean. So . . .

Greg Cool . . . / Huh. That's . . . yeah.

> *She smiles at him and disappears. Greg watches her go.*

SCENE TWO

At work.
　Carly sitting at a table, eating her lunch. Looking up at the clock. After a minute, Greg wanders in with his lunch and a book in one hand – he wears a pair of goggles up on his head tonight. He stops cold, looking at Carly.
　After a beat, he turns around to leave; she stops him by calling out his name.

Carly . . . Greg.

Greg Oh. (*Spins around.*) Hey.

Carly Hi. (*Beat.*) What'cha reading tonight?

Greg Just some . . . Swift. / So, how's it going?

Carly Huh. / You know . . . tired, but that's fine.

Greg Right.

Carly Third's pretty brutal. (*Yawns.*) God!

Greg Yeah.

Carly Don't know how you've done it for so many years . . .

Greg Well, you know, you just . . . keep chugging or whatever. Becomes part of the routine. (*Beat.*) *Or*, as in my case, you leave youself no other options in life . . .

Carly Right!

Greg So, where's Kent?

Carly Home.

Greg Yeah? / He sick or what?

Carly Uh-huh. / No . . .

Greg Haven't seen him for, like, I dunno. All week, seems like.

Carly Mmm.

Greg Our last game, I guess. He's alright?

Carly S'pose so.

Greg 'Kay.

Carly Kent's trying to . . . I mean, he has. He's moved now over to days.

Greg *What?*

Carly Since Thursday. / Yep.

Greg Really? / He didn't tell *me* . . .

Carly No? Thought you guys were best buds . . .

Greg Me, too. Oh, well . . .

Carly They had an opening up on the board.

Greg Right, yeah, I saw that. (*Beat.*) Thought about it myself but, you know . . .

Carly Mmm-hmm, and he applied and got it. It's not as much money, what with the evening differential and all that, but he figures you get more overtime that way, being at a cheaper rate or whatnot.

Greg Huh.

Carly Yep.

Greg OK, cool. Well, I'm gonna head back down there, probably. See ya.

Carly You can sit if you want to . . .

Greg Nah, that's alright. We're busy and I'm really just on a . . . Frozen foods wait for no man, so . . . (*Pulls on goggles.*) See ya.

Carly I'd like to talk to you if that's OK.

Greg Um, sure. (*Points.*) *Officially*, or . . . are there paper towels missing ?

Carly No . . . (*Smiles.*) You can eat, too, if you wanna. I don't want you just staring at me, gonna make me all self-conscious.

Greg Sorry. (*Lifts up goggles.*) Here.

Carly No, it's fine, I'm just – I know what it's like, being on break. / Time's precious.

Greg True. / (*Opens his bag.*) I've been buying my food lately, which stinks. 7-Eleven. Taquitos only get you so far in life . . .

Carly Right!

Greg But I'm terrible about making it myself, so it's better than nothing, I suppose . . .

Carly Steph used to do it, huh?

Greg Always did.

Carly You see her or anything?

Greg Once or twice.

Carly Nice. (*Beat.*) How'd that go?

Greg Pretty well: first time she stood up in public and told me how hideous I was – as a physical specimen, I mean – but the next time was better. She just hit me.

> *Carly studies him, not sure this is true or not. Enough time elapses that it must be and she bursts out laughing.*

Carly Oh *shit* . . .

Greg Yeah, glad you could enjoy that. Really makes the pain worth it . . .

Carly . . . I'm sorry . . .

Greg No, please, go on, the humiliation is nothing compared to the joy it brings you . . .

Carly Shut up! (*Smiles.*) You're funny . . .

Greg Yeah, that's me.

Carly You are, though. I've always thought you had a good sense of humour . . .

Greg Thanks. / Huh.

Carly Yep, you're funny. / You are . . .

Greg Carly, why does this feel like a set-up of some kind here? Hmm?

Carly It's not . . .

Greg Seriously, you haven't, you know, spoken three words in kindness to me since Steph moved away and that's alright, I get that, but you're really throwing me off tonight and I just wanna know where we stand. OK? No offence, but . . .

Carly waits for a moment, studying him. Greg struggles to make eye contact and just manages it.

Carly . . . I need to ask you something.

Greg See? I really am, like, psychic.

Carly It's nothing.

Greg Yeah?

Carly No big deal . . .

Greg Those are sorta famous last words . . . you know? Followed by, 'So, did you kill the guy over in Aisle 13 or not?'

Carly Come *on*, don't always bust my chops about security! It's a *job*. (*Smiles.*) I'm trying to talk to you here . . . please?

Greg OK, OK, sorry. Go for it.

Carly It's about Kent.

Greg I figured . . .

Carly Yeah, and I just want you to tell me the truth here, that's all. 'Cause, well . . . look, you know I'm pregnant . . .

Greg I swear it's not mine . . .

Carly Ass! (*Slaps him, laughing.*) Come on.

Greg Sorry.

Carly . . . And we're, you know, very excited and all that. / We are.

Greg That's . . . / Great.

Carly Yeah, and I'm happy and sad and . . . like, so many different things, all within a twenty-four hour period every day.

Greg I'll bet.

Carly But what I'm not right now, what I don't seem to be able to get to . . . is some place that makes me feel, you know, OK. Safe.

Greg And why's that?

Carly *Umm* . . . why do you think?

Greg I'm guessing Kent . . . but only because of the way you're saying that to me. That's all.

Carly Really?

Greg Yes . . . I'm . . . why? / What's bothering you?

Carly I dunno. / Little things. A change in his routine, this day schedule, and how he's out of the house a lot when I call him – he says he's sleeping but I've asked the neighbours and they say that his car'll be gone sometimes – just stuff.

Greg It's . . . Carly, it's probably nothing.

Carly You know what? 'Probably' is *so* far from being my friend right now . . .

Greg I'm *sure* it's not. / Promise.

Carly Yeah? / Alright.

Greg I mean . . . No, I'm not here on earth to be a, you know, to vouch for Kent, but yeah, I'd put good money on it . . .

Carly OK.

Greg Seriously. / I really would.

Carly Then fine. / Good.

Greg I *so* don't believe you for a second!

Carly HA! Fair enough! You win. (*Beat.*) I want you to do something for me, though, OK? I just want you to look at me for a second. Right at me. It's stupid and all that shit, I know, but I figure if you can look me in the eye and lie then at least I did everything I can do in this situation and you'll be the one who gets to go to Hell . . .

Greg *Thanks* . . .

Carly Hey, I'm carrying the baby, you get to carry the guilt . . .

Greg Super.

Carly So?

Greg What?

Carly You truthfully and with full disclosure do not know anything that's going on with my husband? Any woman that he's seeing or way he's feeling that might suggest he's getting weird on me . . . nothing?

Greg Carly . . .

Carly Answer.

Greg This is not fair . . . Seriously, I'm not one to point fingers or whatever, but this is really not right of you to do to me. It's a no-win, as they like to say . . . a no-way-I-can-come-out-of-this-well situation.

Carly Why's that? I mean, if you're so sure you know him . . .

Greg *Because* . . . he's his own person.

Carly I know that, I *know*, but you've known him for, like . . . ever. So . . .

Greg I'm his friend, I work with the guy, but that doesn't mean I know what's going on up in his head . . . what he's doing when he has a day off or runs down to the store to get you some – I don't know what you're hungry for when you're pregnant, what're you craving these days?

Carly Candy mostly. Sweets.

Greg Ha! OK, so I'm sure he's doing what he is supposed to be doing and thinking a bunch of lovely thoughts about his wife and the mother of his kid as he picks you up that Ben and Jerry's . . . I'm sure that's the case.

Carly I'm not saying he's not . . .

Greg Good, because I'm almost one-hundred-and-ten per cent sure that's the story . . . *but* I am not his priest, I don't see into the *heart* of Kent like an old-time prophet . . .

Carly You're a really good bullshitter, do you know that?

Greg Yeah, totally.

Carly Fine.

Greg I'm just saying. You can't ask me that . . . and not because I know anything, because I . . . I'm ignorant here. Really. / (*Smiling.*) You're talking to the wrong guy . . .

Carly I see. / (*Beat.*) And if I find something out . . . I mean, if I was to find a, you know, different type of hair on his passenger headrest or, or, like, a photo or something – this receipt from a restaurant he'd been to, with you supposedly, but the price would suggest that another couple people might've been there – what should I do about that?

Greg . . . Listen . . .

Carly No, I mean it. If you were pregnant – just go with me for a second here – imagine it and think it through with me . . . what'd be your course of action in a moment such as that? Of truth.

Greg If that were to happen . . . *if* you had come upon something like that, either by you looking for it or by accident, I'd ask me outright for the truth and I'd expect to then hear it. / That's what I'd do – if you were to really, you know, decide to make this the most *excruciating* break that I've lived through. Ever. Then yes.

Carly OK. / (*Laughs.*) Alright then . . .

Greg You good?

Carly Yeah . . .

Greg pats her on the shoulder and stands up, grabbing up his garbage with him. Heads to the can.

Greg . . . And I'm really happy for you guys, about the baby. / I am.

Carly Thanks. / We're hoping for a *shortstop* . . . / once we get the sonogram, I mean. / Yeah.

Greg Great! / So right field is still mine? / Well, see ya . . .

He nods and starts for the door – Carly stops him cold.

Carly . . . So I'm asking you then.

Greg What?

Carly That question. The one that you'd ask if you were pregnant and wondering about all this . . . stuff . . .

Greg Carly . . . (*Beat.*) I've seen Kent, like, *two* times in the last month. If that. So, I'm not sure I'm the guy to . . . but yeah, we've been out to dinner once in that time. / We decided to splurge and . . . eat over at that Italian joint out by the lake –

Carly OK. / 'Visconti's'?

Greg That's the one. My idea. / (*Laughs.*) Turns out . . . guess what? I run into Steph out there, with some guy. / Yeah. Unbelievable.

Carly Huh. / Wow.

Greg So, anyway, that's . . .

Carly This was from Longhorn's, the rib place. Over on 22nd.

Greg No, I know that, I know, I'm just saying that's where we started out, the Italian. So I see Stephanie and we talked – that's the time she whacked me one – and so when they get there we decide to not deal with all that business and just go get a rack of ribs over there. At, you know. Yeah. We did that. That's what we decided to . . . you know. End up doing. Us. / All of us.

Carly OK. / I see. Except for, like, the main part – the 'us' part. The 'us' of it all. How many other 'us's were there? Hmm?

Greg Oh, right, right! Sorry . . . this is making me a little, sorry. Friends of ours, from day shift. We all met up – don't see them very often – and we had dinner. / Simple.

Carly OK. / Girls or guys?

Greg Guys – after the ball game. It's the same date as a game day, you can check it on a calendar. (*Beat.*) It's the truth . . .

Carly Uh-huh. Same truth that Kent'd tell me if I called him up right now? Here, in front of you?

Greg . . . Yes. (*Beat.*) Absolutely. Two guys. You want their names?

Carly No. Then alright. I'm . . . it's OK then.

Carly cries suddenly, a burst of tears, followed quickly by laughter. Then more. Stops. Wipes her eyes.

Shit, I don't know if I can take another six months of this, you know?!

Greg *Me* either! (*Grins.*) You run a pretty tight little investigation there, *Mrs Columbo*.

Carly Thanks. / (*Smiles.*) Sorry for the . . . sorry!

Greg 'S OK. / Not a problem. Honestly.

She gathers her stuff and walks to the garbage – tosses it out. Starts to walk past Greg and then, suddenly, pivots around and grabs him, hugging him tightly. He returns it.

Carly I don't know why God had to make it so, like . . . *hard* to trust you guys. But he did. And it sucks . . .

A loud buzzer goes off. Carly exits. After a moment, Greg sits down and pulls out his cell phone. He stares at it.

Greg suddenly lashes out and kicks a chair against the table. Smash! He shakes his head, then makes a call.

A moment with Carly.

Carly . . . I'm very attractive. I am. I've always been that way but it's no great big deal to me – if anything, it's worked *against* me for most of my life. (*Beat.*) Example: have you ever tried to walk through some store, a supermarket, you're in a hurry and you're moving along – picking up some milk or an item or two like that – while some guy is following you the whole time around the place? Seriously, with a cart and maybe even a kid in it but he keeps showing up in the same sections you're in, or you can see him way down the other end, just *coincidentally* passing through the spots that you're in. For, like, a half-dozen aisles in a row. (*Beat.*) And that's not all because he finds a way to get in the same check-out as you and to do the small talk and even tries to help you out to the car, whatever he can do. It's weird and gross and upsetting, it's enough to make you throw up sometimes – I've done that before, pulled over and vomited by the roadside – all 'cause some man made me so nervous. I've then been followed, too. Yeah. Not just out to my car but all the way home . . . slowly going along behind me to see where I live. Or work. Or through the mall, from store to store, by people. This happens so much, I mean, not like every day, but enough that I couldn't even give you a number. In my lifetime. And for what? Because I'm great or smart or have this, this wonderful and witty way about me? No. How could

71

anybody know that from chasing me around Safeway?
The answer is – they couldn't. Nothing to do with me,
that's what the truth of it is. It's about this . . . (*Points.*)
My face. I was born with it, people, that's all. (*Beat.*)
Listen, I'm not saying I don't understand how I got lucky
in many ways, I do get that, I *do*, I just want folks to
know that beauty comes with a price, just like ugly does.
Different ones, of course, and I'll take what I've got, but
I've cried myself to sleep at night because of who *I* am as
well, and you should know that . . . (*Beat.*) I'm sorry,
didn't mean to get all heavy or anything, but I do think
about shit like that sometimes. My shift at work's kinda
long, you know? It is – so I've usually got some time on
my hands to, you know . . . whatever. Think, I guess.

SCENE THREE

At the ball field.
 *Kent is dressed in baseball pants and socks. Team shirt
that is work-related. He's stretching – has his shoes off.*

Kent That's it, Rich. Hammer it home. Fuckin' douche.

*After a moment, Greg enters. Same kind of gear but
not so serious. Plops down near Kent – attempts a few
warm-ups.*

Greg Hey, man. Why're you warming up way over here?

Kent Helps me focus. (*Beat.*) What's up?

Greg Didn't know if you were gonna make it today, with
the new schedule and all.

Kent Nah, I'm still free on Saturdays – you keep your
seniority even if you move.

Greg Ahhh. That's cool. (*Beat.*) Never told me, so . . .
last to know and all that.

Kent . . . Sorry. No big deal – not like we're in a *relationship* or something . . . (*Smiles.*) Can't miss this, dude, it's a *playoff* game! Want that trophy.

Greg Well, good, then, least we'll have the infield covered . . .

Kent You know it – but Rich is pitching so that fucks up the whole thing. Wish he'd let someone else have a shot at the mound . . .

Greg Me, too. I'd even try it; not that I'm a pitcher, mind you, but hey . . . don't think it could hurt.

Kent Exactly! Guy's arm is total crap. (*Grins.*) Seriously – stuffed with, like, dog shit.

They laugh together at this – they keep working out.

Greg So . . . what's new? / You happy?

Kent Nada. / Big question there, buddy . . .

Greg Yeah, but, you know, I mean . . .

Kent Like with what?

Greg I dunno. About the baby and all that.

Kent Sure, that's cool, I guess.

Greg Good.

Kent Carly's getting kinda tubby but it's sort of cute, too. Never seen her with an ass like that before . . .

Greg Huh.

Kent I'll put up with it, though. For now.

Greg Right.

Kent Long as she hits the gym, like, *day* after she delivers, we're all fine . . .

Greg That's nice.

Kent Hey, she says it louder than me . . . Carly knows that's all she's got going so she's gonna take care of it. Her looks. (*Beat.*) Dude, beautiful women are like athletes: couple good years and then the knees go.

Greg Whatever. (*Beat.*) You pick out a name yet?

Kent Nope, too early – use my *mom's*, probably. We had that test – it's a fucking girl.

Greg Alright . . . Anyway, it's good to see you, man. Miss you on nights.

Kent Wish I could say the same, bro. It is *so* sweet being off by three and sleeping like a white man, fuck! You know?

Greg Course.

Kent Awesome . . . plus, feel like I've got more time to myself. / Evenings free.

Greg Uh-huh. / I wouldn't know . . .

Kent That's because you suck. You just keep working for 'da man' like a fucking *coolie*.

Greg Ha! (*Laughs.*) I'm just used to it.

Kent That's true. (*Grins.*) You've sucked for years . . .

Greg throws his cap at Kent, who ducks and smiles. Silence.

Hey, by the way . . . thanks for, you know, whenever that was. Very cool.

Greg What's that?

Kent Covering for me. About Crystal.

Greg Oh, right, yeah . . .

Kent 'Preciate it. (*Grins.*) Quite a *tale* you came up with there. Pretty good!

Greg Uh-huh.

Kent You've afforded me some very, well, just *amazing* times – thanks to you doing that . . . (*Beat.*) Carly heads to work now and over comes Crystal. Bam! / Or me there.

Greg Huh. / I'm sure.

Kent Doing shit that'd make your head spin, I bet . . . never seen a girl like this one!

Greg Wow.

Kent Something else. *Nasty*, really, but in a fun way, too, you know? / Sexy-dirty.

Greg Sure. / That's great . . .

Kent It's different, anyhow. *In*ventive.

Kent smiles, starts pulling on his cleats. Greg yawns.

Greg Look, about that . . . your . . .

Kent Yeah?

Greg I don't think I can, I mean, don't ask me to help out with that any more, OK?

Kent What?

Greg Your secrets there, whatever you're doing with that girl.

Kent Crystal.

Greg Yes, her.

Kent She's got a name, Greg . . . even if she does like taking Polaroids of my cock.

Greg That's . . . I really never needed to know a fact like that, Kent.

Kent Yeah, but now you do . . . and I take 'em of her, too. / *Loads* of 'em.

Greg Super. / Hmm. Didn't even know she had a cock. Learn a little something every day.

Kent Ha! 'S not really that funny, dude . . .

Greg Well . . . anyhow, don't ask me to do that again, alright? 'Cause I'm . . . I can't. I just . . .

Kent You mean you won't.

Greg No, I'm saying . . . yeah, maybe. Won't.

Kent Right, 'cause of course you can – you can do most anything you want, so it stands to reason that you could if you wanted to. If you *had* to help your friend, or, like, felt inclined to, then you could without any problems . . . so you *won't* do it, that's what you're really saying. / You *will* not.

Greg O-kay. / Yes.

Kent I see . . .

Greg I just, you know . . . I felt like shit when I did that to Carly. Even though we don't always get along – it was crappy, it was, and I don't wanna be that guy to her any more, alright? / I'm – this isn't being judgemental or saying anything about your lifestyle or whatnot, I'm just saying it needs to quit for me. Being that guy.

Kent Hey, fine. / I get it.

Greg Then good.

Kent Whatever you gotta do. / Or not.

Greg Right. / Yep.

Kent Yep. (*Beat.*) I mean, you're in it now, but you don't have to do any more if it bugs you so much . . .

Greg What does that mean? 'In it'?

Kent Nothing.

Greg No, seriously, what?

Kent Just that, you know . . . you helped make it happen, the first place. / When I brought it up . . . *Yes* . . .

Greg No, I didn't. / No . . .

Kent Yeah, you said, 'Go for it' when we were talking in the break room. / I remember it specifically, and so that's what I did . . .

Greg But . . . no, that was . . . / That was *before* . . .

Kent And you went out to dinner with us, lied to my wife about it, practically *took* the pictures for us – but if you suddenly got a case of the conscience, then fine.

Greg Look, you do what you want – your life's a different thing than mine and if you can do that, realistically live with yourself after you act that way, then it's OK . . .

Kent Hey, man, thanks, I really appreciate you giving me your *permission* here . . .

Greg I'm just saying . . . it's . . .

Kent And I'm saying this: don't be such a lump of shit, OK? / Not some high-minded guy who sits in judgement on his friends . . .

Greg Look . . . / I'm not.

Kent That's *exactly* what you're doing!

Greg No, Kent, I'm not, I'm saying that I just can't be a party to lying right now, to a bunch of secrets or that sorta deal where I'm, I'm, I'm put in that position . . .

Kent Whatever, man.

Kent pulls out a roll of tape and roughly tears some off; begins to wrap it round his wrists.

Greg It's pretty easy – we don't see each other that much right now, I have no idea what you're doing out there at night or, you know, two *hours* from now, so . . . you keep it to yourself and we're not gonna have any problems. / Agreed?

Kent . . . Fine. / Sure. God – know what you are?

Greg No, what?

Kent What you sound exactly like when you're talking like that?

Greg I don't, no.

Kent A fucking pussy. That's what.

Greg Great . . .

Kent You do, though, *exactly* like the kind of frightened little pussy that I used to beat the shit outta back in school. / Yeah, come over here and say that.

Greg I remember – 'S *half* the reason I became your friend; so you didn't do it to me. / Oh, good, that'll really be perfect for team spirit, if you and I get in a fight now.

Kent We won't, don't worry.

Greg Good . . .

Kent 'Cause you'd never do it, not even in a million years.

Greg 'S that right?

Kent Yeah, it is. 'S completely true.

Greg And why's that?

Kent Because you're as egotistical as the next guy and you wouldn't want me kicking your ass in front of all these people that you know . . .

Greg Oh, *really?*

Kent Pretty much. (*Beat.*) Guys like you always talk big but that's about it . . .

> *A Mexican stand-off – Kent standing still as Greg slowly sizes him up. Finally, Greg goes and retrieves his hat.*

Greg No, I'm not gonna do that . . .

Kent Good for you. Smart.

Greg Get into that kinda thing with you, and not because I'm scared.

Kent I'll bet.

Greg I'm *not.* (*Beat.*) I'm walking away from it because that's what a grown-up does. OK? / No!! Because *real* men don't have to wail away on each other to prove some . . . point . . .

Kent *And* because you're a faggot. / Whatever you think, dude . . .

Greg Well, that's what I'm choosing to do, to forget it and head over to right field. Let it go . . . / (*To himself.*) I mean, you cheat on her, you're jealous – it's so fucking *bizarre!* I'm . . .

Kent Su-per. / . . . Don't *worry* about it . . .

Greg Fine. Just remember what I said . . .

Kent Same goes for you. Pussy.

Greg Hey, Kent, knock it off, alright? I've had about enough of your shit – a *decade* or so's right about my limit . . .

Kent What're you gonna do about it? Go tell Carly?

Greg Maybe I will . . .

Kent Bullshit, you don't even have the balls for that. / No way.

Greg No? / You sure?

Kent I *know* you don't. And why? Because you'd hate not being liked, that's why. (*Beat.*) Fact that she'd hold you responsible for part of this – and she would – you couldn't deal with that, and when she tells Steph about it? Shit, you'd cry like the little fucking douchebag that you are . . .

Greg Dude, what is the *matter* with you today?

Kent I guess I'm cleaning house. Realise that I don't really need you in my life . . .

Greg Know what, that's fucking fine with me . . . I feel the *exact* same way! Felt it for *years*, just too goddamn lazy to do anything about it . . .

Kent Good. / That's *very* good, pussy. / Say that to my fucking face.

Greg Yes, it is. / Whatever, asshole. / Oh, God . . .

Greg is trying to think fast – Kent flexes and stands tall.

I mean, Jesus Christ . . . why does 'guy' shit *always* gotta end up like this? With somebody throwing punches . . .

Kent Suck. My. Dick. (*Beat.*) Always acting like you're better than me because why? Huh? / Because you *read*? Fuck that!

Greg Kent . . . / You know what this is? You're not mad at me . . . you're angry at yourself. / You're . . .

Kent What kinda two-dollar philosophy is that, huh? / Why the hell would I be mad at *me*?!

Greg Because of what you're doing. / You're . . .

Kent I *like* what I'm doing! / FUCK YOU!!

Kent grabs Greg and drops him to the ground. Lands on top of him.

Greg Get off me . . . bastard . . . Awww! Oww!!

Kent Then shut up . . . / *Stop* . . .

Greg No, I'm not gonna . . . / *You* stop . . .

Kent Shut up, shut up, SHUT THE FUCK UP!

Kent draws back to punch Greg in the face – Greg struggles to cover himself up. After a moment, Kent pushes off him and stands up. Dusts himself clean.

Could care less what you fucking think about it! Dick . . .

Greg Fine. God, you're . . . shit. / Fine.

Kent Yeah. / 'Fine'.

Greg Just . . . always knew you were a fucking *hot head*, but . . . holy shit . . . (*Beat.*) Like some goddamn bully, I can't even believe it . . . supposed to be a grown man and you're up in my face like a fifth-grader. Jesus!

Kent Oh, and as long as we're getting it all out here, our feelings and all that . . . might as well let you in on something.

Greg What's that?

Kent You sure? / Huh? (*Moves closer.*) You *sure*?

Greg Dude, just – whatever. / (*Stands up to him.*) You better back the hell up, man . . .

Kent Your ex is an ugly piece a' shit. / Real fucking Alpo eater that I never understood your interest in . . .

Greg Shut your mouth . . . / Kent! STOP!!

Kent Not that it's my business or whatever . . . I'm just telling you what I always felt about 'er. (*Beat.*) Plain as a barn door and everybody says that, not just me. / Goddamn *laughing stock* at work . . . I mean, shit, man, your taste in women is, like, completely up your ass! It's . . .

Greg You're . . . / You are a . . . motherfucker . . .

Kent It's a fact – only reason anybody'd be with her is 'cause she gives good head. People been saying that for ever . . . (*He picks up his mitt and turns.*) Fuck it. I gotta go get ready . . .

    Kent stops cold when Greg's mitt hits him in the back.

Please don't make me humiliate you twice in one day, buddy . . .

Greg Fuck. You. (*Beat.*) Talk about someone that I care about like that, then I say 'Fuck you, Kent.' Ya hear me? Huh?! *Shithead.*

    Greg pulls off his team shirt and throws it on the ground.

Kent Hey, man, what're you doing? We've only got *nine* guys . . . / Wait, hold up . . .

Greg This team is bullshit. / I'm outta here.

Kent You can't do that! You signed up – guys're gonna be pissed! Come on, it's a *playoff*! We can't do it without a full squad . . . / Dude, no, you can't fucking . . . I can't get somebody else over here now; they gotta be *registered* over at the Y!

Greg Too bad . . . / Then you're fucked. Sorry.

Kent Greg . . . Listen, you prick! Don't!

Greg You explain it to 'em. / Go ahead, go on.

Kent How the fuck am I gonna do that? / *How?!*

Greg . . . Show 'em a Polaroid of your *dick*.

Greg picks up his athletics bag and leaves. Kent explodes forward and confronts him – blocks his exit.

Kent You're not going anywhere, dude, except on the field! I'm done messing with you!

Greg Kent, get out of my way . . .

Kent Fuck you! / Get that jersey back on!!

Greg I mean it, man . . . / I'm not kidding.

Kent DO IT! NOW!! (*Pushes him.*) I'm serious. Take a *fuck*load more than the likes of you to ruin my chances at that trophy . . .

Greg Alright, fine . . . We'll do this here for everybody to see, I don't care, but we need to be totally clear about what's gonna happen . . . OK? / O-KAY?

Kent Whatever, bitch. / Go on . . .

Greg calmly steps up against his friend and smiles, with a kind of stillness falling over him. Kent steps back.

Greg I'm gonna do this – you and me – but it's not just because of what you said about Steph. *This* is gonna happen because you need it. For *who* you are and *what* you've done and, and . . . just *all* the shit you will no doubt perpetrate over the rest of your life on unsuspecting people – today *and* in the . . . upcoming future. OK? / THAT is why.

Kent What the fuck? / Eat shit, asswipe.

Before Kent can react, Greg unleashes a flurry of punches that drop Kent in his tracks. He goes down hard. Frankly, Kent proceeds to get his ass kicked. Rather soundly.

After a moment, Greg gets up and gathers his stuff. Walks off. Kent staggers to his feet a bit later. Calling out.

Dude, come on – COME ON! Fuck!! You are such a fucking . . . fuck!! You dick!! That is so . . . shit, shit, shit, shit! FUCK!! Try that again, I dare ya! You hear me? DARE-YOU! Fucking *sneak* attack . . .

Kent proceeds to kick the shit out of Greg's jersey – like a toddler unleashing his fury on a stuffed animal.

EEEEAAAAAWWWW!! You fucking . . . suck, man! You *totally* do. Suck cock. *Big* time.

Spent now, Kent stops his rant and kicks at the dirt with his cleats. Huffs and puffs. Stamps his foot – in case you didn't notice, it's a full-blown tantrum.

Looks over and notices a group of folks (unseen) watching.

The fuck are you *guys* looking at?! Huh?! Mind your own goddamn business . . . Shit!

Kent checks to make sure the others are gone. Paces. He kicks Greg's uniform once more for emphasis.

Stupid . . . GOD!! (*Spits.*) Fucking *child*.

He remains where he is, unsure of what to do next.

SCENE FOUR

At work.

Carly sitting at a table, eating by herself. Just getting ready to finish. She stands up – she's showing even more now.

Greg enters with an apple and a book. He smiles at Carly; she gives him a little hug and moves towards the door.

Carly Hi there.

Greg Morning. / Even though it's *night* out.

Carly Yep. / (*Smiles.*) Right . . . or 'siesta'.

Greg 'Raspberry'! (*Grins.*) You feeling OK?

Carly Pretty much. Puffy. Bloated. The size of a milk cow, I guess, but OK.

Greg Ha! (*Makes a sound.*) Moooo!

Carly God, you don't have to agree.

Greg Sorry.

Carly You dick.

Greg No, seriously. You're the most beautiful cow out there. / Don't forget that, OK? And I'm *including* your face . . .

Carly *Thanks*. / (*Smiles.*) I'm sure there must be a compliment wedged in there somewhere . . .

Greg There is. Trust me.

Carly I do. (*Grins.*) Must be the uniform, huh? You guys always go for a woman in blue. Kent does anyway. / Least that's what he says . . .

Greg Yeah. / Mmmm.

Carly OK, well . . . enjoy your break.

Greg Will do. 'Nother two hours, huh? We can make that . . .

Carly Yep.

Greg Hey Carly, you got any sick time or anything built up?

Carly Sure. / Have to, what with the baby coming and everything . . . Did Kent tell you we're gonna call her 'Jennifer'?

Greg Cool. / No, that's . . . (*Beat.*) Know what you should do? Seriously?

Carly What's that?

Greg Take off – just tell your supervisor that you're feeling sick and go home. Jump in bed with Kent and surprise him.

Carly . . . You think?

Greg Absolutely. / I bet he'd love that.

Carly Huh. / Maybe I will . . . one of these days.

Greg I mean tonight, even. Be good for him.

Carly 'Kay. I'll think about it . . .

Greg No, *tonight*. / I'd really do it now if I were you . . . *right* now. / Honestly, you should go.

Carly Oh. / (*Starts to cry.*) OK. / I'll, umm . . . yeah . . . I'll just . . .

> One last look at Greg and she is gone. Greg gets a drink, sits down at a table. Cracks open his book and reads.

After a moment, Steph wanders in through the door. She's all fancied up but wearing a coat over her clothes.

Steph . . . Hey you.

Greg Steph? / (*Surprised.*) Hi.

Steph Hello. / You OK?

Greg Uh-huh. (*Beat.*) Did you . . . You just missed Carly. / Uh-huh, she was . . . I mean . . .

Steph Really? / That wasn't . . . was that *her*? Just a second ago?

Greg Yep.

Steph Wow. Holy *shit* . . . (*Gesturing.*) Her ass is, like . . . damn! / Good! That girl deserves a big ass for once . . .

They have a good laugh about that. It builds for a moment.

Greg Yeah. / So, this is . . . huh. What's up?

Steph Nothing, I just . . . who you reading now?

Greg Oh, just, umm, Washington Irving. / Uh-huh. (*Beat.*) You want anything? I can . . .

Steph Ahhh, 'Rip Van Winkle'. That's a good one. Sad, though . . . / No, that's fine.

Greg Alright. (*Beat.*) Sorry you missed Carly . . .

Steph That's OK. We're staying in touch, so no biggie. Online and stuff. / Skyping.

Greg Cool. / Great.

Steph . . . Anyway, I came to see you.

Greg looks Steph up and down – she can't meet his eyes.

Don't. Please. *Stare.*

Greg Why not? You're all dressed up . . .

Steph I dunno, I'm just . . .

Greg And I like looking at you.

Steph Yeah?

Greg Always did.

Steph Not enough, though, right?

Greg No, that was not . . . *No*, Steph. You got that into your head, was told a stupid thing, but no . . . You have a great face. Lots of . . . *character* and, and, you know . . . (*Beat.*) Fuck. I never say the right thing!

Steph No, but thanks. (*Beat.*) Look, I'm . . . I . . .

She searches around for the right word – Greg takes her by hand. Gently.

Greg It's the ring, right? Why you're here?

Steph You *saw* that?

Greg Yeah. Just now.

Steph Oh.

Greg Hey . . . told you before, I'm psychic.

Steph Right. / (*Smiles.*) You did.

Greg Yep. / Sooo . . . lemme guess . . . the 'miserable shithead' turned out to be OK.

Steph You got it.

Greg How OK?

Steph Really pretty damn OK, actually.

Greg Then great. I'm happy for you. (*Beat.*) You should expect goldfish as a wedding gift.

Steph Ha! (*Laughs.*) Excellent . . . Tim's his name. Tim.

Greg Good a name as any, I guess.

Steph (*smiles*) He works with computers . . .

Greg Nice. Can he get me wireless?

Steph slugs Greg a good one on the arm, just for old times' sake. He smiles.

That's the Stephanie I remember!

Steph Idiot . . .

Greg That's me.

Steph The psychic idiot.

Greg Yeah, but once I go back to college and get my degree you're gonna have to call me *Mr* Idiot, so . . . be prepared. Respect is just around the corner . . .

Steph You serious? About college?

Greg Looks like it . . . can't pack boxes all my life. / Much as I *adore* it . . .

Steph No? / Guess not.

A loud buzzer goes off. Greg smiles and points overhead. Steph nods and inches closer to him.

Greg Well, I could, but eventually I'd have to buy a rifle and come through here killing everybody and that just seems excessive.

They grow silent and just look at each other for a bit. Greg reaches over and touches the ring.

Steph We haven't set a date yet.

Greg 'Kay. Lemme know.

Steph (*grins*) Oh, guess, what? I'm a *manager* now. / And you? How's everything?

Greg Yeah? Awesome. / Ohhh, you know . . .

Steph No, I don't. Not really. You were never very good about talking to me – keeping me up-to-date on your life or anything.

Greg True . . .

Steph It's not a cut, it's not . . . just telling you a fact is all. / Kinda secretive.

Greg I *know*. I did, like . . . well, a lot of shit wrong, Steph. / Yeah, I'm aware of that.

Steph Too late, though, right? To fix it?

Greg Prob'ly. You know, 'old dog, new tricks'.

Steph Sure.

Greg Umm . . . so, yeah, I'm gonna try the college thing again.

Steph Oh, yeah?

Greg In September. And I might transfer over to the Edgewater Plant in a few months. We'll see. Maybe just quit altogether. (*Beat.*) I'm no longer playing on the baseball team . . .

Steph Really?

Greg Yep, that's over . . . and, oh, here's a good one – I think I ruined Carly's life. Just before you got here . . .

Steph Is that right?

Greg Maybe. / I didn't mean to, but . . .

Steph Oh. / Nah, I bet you didn't.

Greg You don't know . . .

Steph If it's what I think it is, then no. It's been a long time coming and she'll be two thousand times better because of it. *Lots* better, honestly . . .

Greg You think so?

Steph I would be. (*Thinks.*) Yes. She'll be fine, she's a strong person.

Greg Yeah, I've come to realise that.

Steph Totally.

She nods at this, letting her thoughts float through the air for a moment. Greg watches her.

Greg You really do . . . look . . .

Steph Thanks. I mean, I know I'm just 'regular' and everything, but I can clean up once in a while. / So listen, this is hard for me, to come here and . . . to see you.

Greg Steph, that's . . . / I understand.

Steph But I felt I had to, you know? He put the ring on my finger and it was, like, this amazing moment and I'm crying and so, so happy and all that, but the whole time – all while we're talking about our lives and how we want a house and kids – you're in my head. / Yeah. I'm seeing *you.*

Greg Oh. / Wow. That's . . . I mean . . .

Steph I imagine those same things, all these *things* that Tim is saying to me but I'm picturing them with you because that's how it was in my mind for so long.

Greg Stephanie, I'm . . . / Listen . . .

Steph Just let me *finish.* / (*Softer.*) Please . . .

Greg Sure. Go on.

She turns to Greg now, taking his hand in hers. A smile.

Steph Can't believe I'm even about to say this shit . . . You know, *part* of me is still waiting for you to sweep me off my feet or something, some last-ditch thing to win me back. / (*Elbows him.*) Bastard . . .

Greg Oh. / (*Grins.*) *Really?*

Steph Course! Maybe like some deal outta the movies . . . you know? I mean, why not? If anybody might deserve it that'd be me, after how I got treated . . . / Anyway . . .

Greg The whole thing was a *mis*understanding, Steph, I *promise* you! / I never said . . .

Steph Yeah, well, whatever . . . (*Beat.*) Doesn't matter because the other side of me, the reliable part, was screaming 'Thank God ya came to your fucking *senses!*'

She looks over at Greg to gauge how this has landed. He nods his head but doesn't say anything. Fidgets a bit.

Anyway, look. We're right where we should be now, I really believe it. / I don't want to believe it, that we could've been doing shit to hurt each other but I wrestled with all this stuff over the last few months and, just, I know now that we were not very perfect as a couple.

Greg Maybe. / Yeah, that's kinda fair, I guess.

Steph Not that we weren't good together because we were, I know that, but be honest . . . you were never gonna give me what I have now – this ring or the sort of future I'm wanting from a guy. Right? You do understand that I've thought of you that way, Greg, hoped that you could be that person to me? But you weren't. / Not really.

Greg No. / That's probably . . . (*Beat.*) I'm sorry, Steph, but it's true – I liked you a lot, obviously, even loved you but I was just drifting, and the four years we've spent together probably could've gone on for another four or ended in a *month* and I'd've been fine either way. Really. If ya think back and you're honest about it . . . I don't want you to hit me so I'm hedging my bets here, but look, you know I'm . . . I'm . . .

Steph No, you're . . . that's totally dead on.

Greg Hey, you're free to disagree. If you want to say I'm the greatest guy *ever*, I'm not gonna fight you on it . . .

Steph Oh yeah! (*Grins.*) No chance, buddy.

Greg Figures.

Steph No, you're right. I was the first to say something, but it could've just as easily been you.

Greg Right.

Steph And I know I'm putting all this fucking *moon glow* on it now, like it was special and all . . . but . . . it was just normal.

Greg No, it was special. / Steph, it was, but . . .

Steph What*ever*. / I'm just saying – I'm making it far better in my head than we were. (*Beat.*) I don't even know why I'm here! I don't. Or why I kept hanging on for so long, a whole lot longer than I should've. Fuck! But I love you, Greg, so much . . . I did. And that's not . . . that doesn't make me stupid or . . . whatever. Pathetic. I was just hopeful. I'm a hopeful person and I think that's nice.

Steph looks over at Greg, who wants to say something.

Greg Yeah . . . (*Beat.*) But it wasn't your face; I mean, just so you know, I wasn't ever this, like, 'ass' man or, or some 'legs' guy . . . I like how you looked. Period.

Steph OK, that helps, because, I dunno, it just does . . . (*Beat.*) I maybe shouldn't make such a big deal out of it but it is. To most girls it honestly is. (*Beat.*) Ya know, this guy I have now – he looks at me and that's it. He just *lights* up inside.

93

Greg Good. No, that's good. (*Touches her.*) So go be happy then. / Yes, *that's* what I want for you . . .

Steph Yeah? / Really?

Greg Why not? I'm sure it's possible – you read about it all the time . . .

He reaches over and gives Steph a little sort of hug.

Steph Well, point me in the right direction, would ya?

Greg Sure. It's right over there somewhere . . . / (*Points towards the window.*) Next to that dude in the convertible.

Steph 'Kay. / Ha! Thank you.

Greg No problem. Steph, you look really *pretty*.

Steph Thanks. That's nice. You're still an asshole but I'm gonna miss you . . .

Greg I know you will.

Steph Yeah? How do you know that?

Greg Told you – I'm psychic.

Steph Ha! (*Smiles.*) *Prick* . . .

Greg . . . See? I knew you were gonna say that.

Steph leans forward now, moving slowly towards a kiss. Greg meets her halfway. A lovely moment. Steph starts to cry but catches herself – grabs up her purse and exits.

   Greg goes to the window, looking out. Watching her go.

   He returns to the table and sits. Greg exhales sharply as he puts his head in his hands.

   Another buzzer sounds sharply in the distance.

   He pulls out his book and begins to read.

A buzzer sounds sharply in the distance.
Without looking up, Greg lifts his middle finger up on one hand and flips 'the bird', holds it a moment. Drops it.
Greg leans back, puts his feet up on the table. He goes back to his reading.

A moment with Greg.

Greg . . . What'd I learn from this – all that's happened to me? Shit, I dunno. Nothing, probably, which is my usual pattern. I have no doubt learned absolutely nothing and will be able to apply none of these life lessons to my actual . . . day-to-day routine. Sad but true . . . (*Smiles.*) Just being silly, sorry. No, I'll tell you what I really got a better sense of in these last months, what I learned was this.

A bell sounds. Softer than the work buzzer.

Jesus . . . can't get away from that shit, huh? (*Points.*) I'm in class now, and I'm taking a Humanities elective, no biggie, but we're going over all these paintings, learning a bit about them, and this one sticks in my mind. I mean, after all that happened to . . . you know. It's by this guy Velazquez, and it has a name like – I'm not kidding here – 'The Toilet of Venus' or something. Yeah! And the teacher was going on and on about it, trying to keep us from staring at this lady's bare ass in the picture . . . and he says that the reason we can't really see the woman's face in the mirror – a little cherub-guy is holding the thing so it's hard to see – the *reason* is because we all have a different perception of what real beauty is. Isn't that funny? He's saying it's 'subjective' and that none of us are wrong . . . it's just about personal feelings and stuff. And, see, that's *all* I was ever trying to say to Steph about . . . whatever! What happened. It's all very subjective and we shouldn't worry about that shit . . . that's what I think; and yet I come out like, I dunno, a bit of a bad guy from the whole deal. Life is crazy, right? Yep. (*Beat.*) But the truth of the matter, the honest thing about this is, I think I'm a better man now, after Stephanie. I really do. Not, like, *awesome* or anything, not like that, but at least . . . 'decent', maybe. Yeah. I think she helped make me better. (*Beat.*) I think that I'm . . . I mean, when I start dating again – I'm not now, but when I do – I think I'll be less judgemental about what a person is like. Seriously. I mean, just to be clear, I'm not dating *anybody* right now – thought I should take a little breather on that front! – but I just mean in theory. In *theory* I now know better how to treat people. Like, girls. Or women – I guess they like it when you say 'women'.

Another bell sounds. Greg checks his watch. Smiles.

Steph got married two weeks ago. Yeah. She shifted the dates three times, which made me laugh, but it was finally held a couple Sundays ago. I got invited, too, which was cool. I sat by Carly, actually, and her daughter – who is . . . Kent was a no-show – interesting . . . And it was really . . . Steph looked great. You know? With one of those veils and how brides do . . . with her hair and all . . . She passed me, as her dad was walking her up the aisle, and I got a chance to lean in as she passed and whisper to her, I said, 'Hey . . . you look really beautiful,' and her eyes got all, you know . . . I'm glad I got to say that to her. It was nice.

Greg stops and considers this for a moment. Nodding.

Maybe that's the best thing I realised from my life with her, you know? Steph. Is to always take the time to do that – don't miss out on it because life is so, so fucking short . . . (*Beat.*) I mean, what does it take to be nice every once in a while? Huh? I'll tell you what, not much. (*Beat.*) Hardly anything at all . . .

    Greg starts to say something else but stops himself.
He smiles, nods and wanders off.
    Lights snap off.

End.